THE LEGEND OF
SLEEPY HOLLOW

Book by Helen Watts

Music and lyrics by Eamonn O'Dwyer

⫼SAMUEL FRENCH⫼

FOR AMATEUR PRODUCTION ENQUIRIES

UNITED KINGDOM AND WORLD
EXCLUDING NORTH AMERICA
licensing@concordtheatricals.co.uk
020-7054-7200

Each title is subject to availability from Concord Theatricals, depending upon country of performance.

MUSIC USE NOTE

Licensees are solely responsible for obtaining formal written permission from copyright owners to use copyrighted music in the performance of this play and are strongly cautioned to do so. If no such permission is obtained by the licensee, then the licensee must use only original music that the licensee owns and controls. Licensees are solely responsible and liable for all music clearances and shall indemnify the copyright owners of the play(s) and their licensing agent, Concord Theatricals, against any costs, expenses, losses and liabilities arising from the use of music by licensees. Please contact the appropriate music licensing authority in your territory for the rights to any incidental music.

USE OF COPYRIGHT MUSIC

A licence issued by Concord Theatricals to perform this play does not include permission to use the incidental music specified in this copy. Where the place of performance is already licensed by the PERFORMING RIGHT SOCIETY (PRS) a return of the music used must be made to them. If the place of performance is not so licensed then application should be made to the PRS, 2 Pancras Square, London, N1C 4AG (www.prsformusic.com).A separate and additional licence from PHONOGRAPHIC PERFORMANCE LTD, 1 Upper James Street, London W1F 9DE (www.ppluk.com) is needed whenever commercial recordings are used.

IMPORTANT BILLING AND CREDIT REQUIREMENTS

If you have obtained performance rights to this title, please refer to your licensing agreement for important billing and credit requirements.

THE LEGEND OF SLEEPY HOLLOW

First Performed at The Other Palace, London on 22nd August 2018 by The National Youth Music Theatre.

IMOGEN	Hattie Attwood
JOSHUA	Bill Stanley
SABINE	Jade Oswald
FATHER ABRAM	John Prowse
BALTUS VAN FLEET	Alfie Richards
LISBETH VAN FLEET	Emily Hope
KATRINA VAN FLEET	Hayley Canham
HANS VAN RIPPER	Nathan Harter
BROM VAN BRUNT	Joe Usher
EVA VAN BRUNT	Sissy Ford
WILLEM	Tomos Brace-Jenkins
ICHABOD CRANE	George Renshaw
FLORINA	Katie Ramshaw
JOHAN	Markus Harman
Their children: RUTH (10)	Phoebe Connolly
ABEL (12)	Ben Pulford
JAKOB (14)	Bruno Magnanti
MARTHA (14)	Madeleine Banbury
ESTHER (16)	Amelia Lamb
HENRIETTE	Annabel Howe
KLAUS	Dash Buckley
Their children: ISAAC (13)	Spike Maxwell
ANNA (14)	Lottie Beck Johnson
DRIKA	Chloe Twigg
MARKUS	Ciaran O'Brien
Their children: ESPEN (11)	Matteo Elezi
REBEKAH (11)	Amy Mepham
ROSA (14)	Alice Knight
THE INDIAN GIRL	Amy Mepham
POOR LITTLE TOM	Matteo Elezi
MAJOR ANDRE	
PETER'S WIFE	Amelia Lamb
THE HEADLESS HORSEMAN	Alfie Richards

Director	Alex Sutton
Musical Director	Charlie Ingles
Choreographer	Cydney Uffindell-Phillips
Designer	Rebecca Brower
Lighting Designer	Christopher Nairne
Sound Designer	Luke Swaffield for Autograph Sound
Graphic Designer	Rebecca Pitt
Assistant Director	Sam Gaffney
Assistant Musical Director	Jacopo Marai
Assistant Choreographer	Natalie Haslam
Administrator	Cicero Magalhães
Producer for NYMT	Jeremy Walker

Musicians:

Flute/Clarinet/Bass Clarinet/Bassoon	Michael Madigan
Oboe/Cor Anglais	Maddy Wood
Horn	Frances Gordon
Violin	Dylan Edge
Cello	Helen Butcher
Double Bass	Sophie Walker
Harp	Katie Sherratt
Percussion	Sam Levy
Piano	Jacopo Marai

LIST OF MUSICAL NUMBERS

ACT ONE

1.   Prologue – Strange Child – *Company*
1b. The Girl – *Imogen, Joshua*
2.   A Pleasing Land – *Sabine, Company*
3.   The Devil Never Rests – *Company*
3b. Transition – Shall We Gather At The River – *Company*
3c. Transition – Into Van Fleet's – *Company*
4.   The Tale Of The Headless Horseman – *Baltus*
4b. Transition – Homeward – *Company*
5.   Poor Little Tom – *Children*
6.   The New England Primer – *Children*
7.   We Used To Think The Earth Was Flat – *Ichabod*
8.   The Life We Live – *Brom, Tenant Farmers*
9.   All Too Soon – *Eva, Katrina*
10. Mr Crane Says – *Children, Ichabod, Tenant Farmers, Fr Abram*
11. Black-Eyed Susan – *Sabine*
11b. Underscore – Strange Things Do Happen
11c. Transition – The Girl – *Imogen*
12. The Tale of the Whippoorwill – *Katrina*
13. Underscore – After Van Fleet
14. The Promise – *Brom, Markus, Johan, Klaus*
14b. Underscore – Outside the Tavern – *Orchestra*
15. The Tale of Major Andre – *Fr Abram, Company*

ACT TWO

16. The Dream – *Sabine*
16b. Transition – After The Dream – *Sabine*
17. Nothing – *Ichabod, Katrina*
18. The Funeral – *Lisbeth, Katrina, Fr Abram, Drika, Tenant Farmers*
19. The Will – *Baltus*
19b. Underscore – After The Will
20. The Dream (reprise) – The Fight – *Sabine, Brom, Katrina*
21. Peter, Peter, Pumpkin Eater – *Children*
22. Transition – The Schoolroom: The Girl Revealed – *Imogen, Company*
23. The Power – *Lisbeth*

24.   Hallows' Eve: The Headless Horseman – *Company,*
      Van Ripper
24b. Underscore – Party Music – Whippoorwill
25.   The Tale of the Drunkard Jack – *Lisbeth, Markus, Johan,*
      Company
25b. Underscore – Party Music – Peter, Peter
26.   The Letter – *Katrina, Ichabod*
27.   The Hollow Wood – *Sabine*
27b. Underscore – The Haunting
27c. The Horseman – *Company*
28.   The Curse – *Katrina*
29.   Eva Remembers – The Tale Of The Indian Girl – *Eva,*
      Children

AUTHOR'S NOTE

Throughout the show the company act as a chorus, helping Imogen to tell the story of Sleepy Hollow by manipulating and dressing the scenes.

The director and designer should use all theatrical trickery at their disposal to make The Hollow Wood and The Haunting sequences in Act Two as terrifying as possible. The echoes of each song may be performed live, or manipulated and distorted via recorded sound.

This musical was commissioned in 2018 by The National Youth Music Theatre, and was directed by Alex Sutton.

CHARACTERS

ICHABOD CRANE (20s) – The new school teacher. Educated and well-travelled, but skeptical of the superstitions of Sleepy Hollow. He falls in love with Katrina.

BALTUS VAN FLEET (40s) – Landlord of Sleepy Hollow. Misanthropic, and often harsh, but ultimately fair in his business dealings. Tender towards his wife and daughter.

LISBETH VAN FLEET (40s) – Baltus's wife. Elegant, quiet but with a hidden strength that emerges after her husband's death.

KATRINA VAN FLEET (18) – Only daughter of Baltus & Lisbeth Van Fleet. She has a quiet, intelligent nature, but becomes passionate and reckless after falling in love with Ichabod Crane.

BROM VAN BRUNT (20s) – Baltus's estate manager and Katrina's fiancé. A salt-of-the-earth farmer, practical and honest, who becomes hardened by his own sense of duty.

SABINE (40s) – Outcast sister of Lisbeth Van Fleet with an instinctive understanding of nature and the Hollow. A dreamer and a mystic, she foresees the tragedy that is coming to the town.

HANS VAN RIPPER (40s) – Baltus's accountant. A sly and calculating businessman, he uses the confusion in the aftermath of Van Fleet's death to try and assume control of Sleepy Hollow.

FATHER ABRAM (20s) – An idealistic, but somewhat ineffectual man of God. Along with the Tenant Farmers, he orchestrates a cruel prank against Ichabod.

EVA VAN BRUNT (15) – Brom's younger sister, and friend to Katrina.

WILLEM (18) – Clerk to Hans Van Ripper, but also his eyes and ears in the town.

IMOGEN (13) – Narrator of the story in 1833, later revealed to be Katrina and Ichabod's daughter. She has had a dark and isolated upbringing in Sleepy Hollow.

JOSHUA (12) – Bright and inquisitive; later revealed to be Eva's son.

Tenant Farmer Families

HENRIETTE and **KLAUS** (30s–50s) – Henriette is a prim and proper, but rather stuck-up woman, and Klaus her long-suffering husband. In their eyes, their children **ANNA** (14) and **ISAAC** (13) can do no wrong.

FLORINA and **JOHAN** (30s–50s) – A loving, wholesome couple who are often outmaneuvered by their numerous, and quite badly-behaved offspring, **ESTHER** (16), **MARTHA** (14), **JAKOB** (14), **ABEL** (12), and **RUTH** (10).

DRIKA and **MARKUS** (30s–50s) – Slightly down-at-heel compared to the others, Markus likes a drink, and Drika has a reputation as a sharp-tongued gossip. Their children, **ROSA** (14), **ESPEN** (11) and **REBEKAH** (11), are quick-witted like their mother.

Ghosts

THE INDIAN GIRL – A Native American child who was slain by The Headless Horseman.
POOR LITTLE TOM – A little boy who was killed by his mother.
MAJOR ANDRE – A British officer hanged as a spy during the American Revolutionary War.
PETER'S WIFE – An adulterous wife who was murdered and buried in a pumpkin patch.
THE HEADLESS HORSEMAN – A Hessian trooper beheaded during the American Revolutionary War.

TIME

1833 (present) and 1820 (past)

SETTING

All the action takes place in the small town of Sleepy Hollow, a secluded New England village near New York. In the original production British accents were used (as the "American accent" did not become formalized until long after 1833), but this is left to the Director's discretion.

ACT ONE

The Church

Throughout the show the company act as a chorus telling the story of Sleepy Hollow by manipulating and dressing the scenes.

[MUSIC NO 1: "PROLOGUE – STRANGE CHILD"]

Date: 1833.

Sleepy Hollow is a dark place, where the souls of the dead are unable to leave. Everything is black and white and there is a sombre mood.

The silhouette of **THE INDIAN GIRL** *is seen surveying the land and then she is gone.*

IMOGEN *(thirteen) stands in the doorway of the church; her mother's funeral has just finished.* **THE VILLAGERS** *file out past her, muttering amongst themselves.*

NB: The Whippoorwill is a bird native to New England (it is mentioned in the text, also called a Nightjar). Its cries can usually be heard at twilight, but if a full moon shines, the Whippoorwill will sing all night long.

DRIKA
POOR CHILD, POOR THING,

LISBETH
A PITIFUL END TO A PITIFUL BEGINNING.
POOR CHILD

+DRIKA
POOR CHILD

KATRINA
SUCH A QUEER THING ...
HER MOTHER IS COLD IN THE CHURCHYARD,
AND THE GIRL WON'T WEEP, WON'T PRAY, WON'T SING,

KATRINA, DRIKA AND LISBETH
STRANGE CHILD, STRANGE CHILD;

BALTUS
STRANGE TALE.
THIRTEEN YEARS IN THE HOLLOW,
AND WE STILL NEVER HEAR THE WHIPPOORWILL WAIL,

ALL
STRANGE DAYS! STRANGE DAYS!

BUT SINCE EVERYONE'S GUILTY
YOU CAN'T TELL WHO TO BLAME!
THERE ARE CHOICES YOU MAKE
THERE ARE PATHS YOU MUST TAKE
SO YOU LIVE WITH THE FEAR
OR YOU DIE WITH THE SHAME!

Pause.

VAN RIPPER + FLORINA
SMALL SLEEPY TOWN WITH A DARK LITTLE PAST.

ALL, VARIOUSLY
WHEN MEMORIES FADE, THEY LEAVE QUESTIONS WHICH ARE
     STILL UNASKED.
SMALL TOWN, SMALL TOWN, SMALL TOWN
BAD DREAMS:
THE SWEAT ON YOUR BROW,
THE FLICKER OF FLAME,
THE THUNDER OF HOOVES,
THE CALL OF HIS NAME:
ICHABOD CRANE!
ICHABOD CRANE!

IMOGEN

> ICHABOD CRANE ...

Pause.

DRIKA

> STRANGE CHILD, STRANGE THING.
> HER MOTHER IS COLD IN THE CHURCHYARD
> AND STILL THE WHIPPOORWILL
> WON'T SING.

> **IMOGEN** *is staring at her mother's grave.* **JOSHUA** *(twelve) approaches her.*

JOSHUA Mother says you're to come home with us now.

> **IMOGEN** *doesn't look at him.*

> I'm sorry about *your* mother.

IMOGEN No one else is.

JOSHUA Why won't they look at you? The folk in the church. What did you do?

IMOGEN Nothing.

JOSHUA Who is Ichabod Crane?

IMOGEN *(she looks at him for the first time)* Why do you want to know?

JOSHUA I keep hearing them say his name.

IMOGEN You're not from Sleepy Hollow, are you?

JOSHUA No.

> **IMOGEN** *looks back at her mother's grave.*

> What's a Whippoorwill?

IMOGEN It's a bird. The people here believe that the Whippoorwill's song caries the souls of the dead to heaven.

JOSHUA And if it doesn't sing..?

IMOGEN Then the soul stays in Sleepy Hollow forever.

Pause.

[MUSIC NO. 1b: "THE GIRL"]

JOSHUA Please, tell me about Ichabod Crane.

IMOGEN I never knew him.

JOSHUA But it's because of him they won't look at you, isn't it?

IMOGEN He only did what he thought was best. They all did.

JOSHUA Please tell me.

IMOGEN

> MY MOTHER USED TO SAY
> THAT NOTHING IN THE WORLD
> CAN EVER CHANGE WHAT'S TRUE
>
> I'LL TELL YOU WHY THEY FEAR ME
> WHAT THEY SEE WHEN THEY STARE
> BUT SWEAR TO ME,
> IF YOU EVER TELL THIS TALE ...

JOSHUA What?

IMOGEN

> DON'T CHANGE A THING

JOSHUA I swear.

IMOGEN Thirteen years ago... Sleepy Hollow was a different place...

[MUSIC NO. 2: "A PLEASING LAND"]

We are transported thirteen years into the past (Date: 1820); Sleepy Hollow is an idyllic riverside hamlet in glorious colour. Outside the church SABINE *(forty) picks herbs and sings her mystical song. This is taken up by other voices in the company:*

SABINE

> A PLEASING LAND OF DROWSY CHARMS
> OF DREAMS THAT DANCE BEFORE THE HALF-SHUT EYE;

OF GORGEOUS CASTLES IN THE CLOUDS
FOREVER FLOATING ROUND A SUMMER SKY.

ALL

THE RIVER SINGS ITS GRACEFUL AIR,
A CONSTANT VOICE OF SHIFTING HARMONY;
THE HOLLOW HELD IN ITS EMBRACE,
FOREVER SLEEPING IN THE RIVER'S LEA.

SABINE

FOREVER SLEEPING IN THE RIVER'S LEA
FOREVER SLEEPING...

Inside the church – Sunday morning. **FLORINA,** *a farmer's wife, enters with her massive brood of unruly* **CHILDREN.** *Her husband* **JOHAN** *follows behind. Everyone is dressed in their Sunday finest.*

[MUSIC NO. 3: "THE DEVIL NEVER RESTS"]

FLORINA

COME ALONG, COME ALONG. JAKOB!

JAKOB

WHAT?

FLORINA

LEAVE THE CANDLE!

JAKOB

WHY?

He is about to set fire to his sister's hair.

FLORINA *(she blows it out)*

MUST WE?
COME ALONG, COME ALONG;
THE DEVIL NEVER RESTS ON A SUNDAY MORNING!
SETTLE DOWN, SETTLE DOWN;
MARTHA!

MARTHA *is beating her brother with a book.*

MARTHA

WHAT?

FLORINA
IS THAT YOUR BIBLE?

MARTHA
YES.

FLORINA
THEN READ IT.
SETTLE DOWN, SETTLE DOWN AND SAY A PRAYER ...
THE DEVIL NEVER RESTS AND THE DEVIL IS EVERYWHERE!

JACOB *(pulling on her sleeve)* Mother? Mother?

FLORINA *(irritated)* Yes? What is it? *(Distracted by another child sitting in the pew saved for the* **VAN FLEETS***)* Don't sit there, that's for Herr Van Fleet's family!

JACOB Have *you* met the new school teacher?

FLORINA No, no one has. Now hold your tongue and say your prayers.

> **JACOB** *literally holds his tongue saying his prayers.*
> **MARTHA** *hits him on the head with a Bible.*

> **HENRIETTE** *and* **KLAUS** *enter – prim and proper, social climbers – their* **CHILDREN** *perfectly behaved.*

HENRIETTE
TO THE FRONT, TO THE FRONT,
KLAUS! FIND A SEAT, DEAR.

FLORINA
HERE?

> *Offering* **HENRIETTE** *the adjacent pew.*

HENRIETTE
NO, THANK YOU.
TO THE FRONT, TO THE FRONT!

HENRIETTE AND FLORINA *(slyly, at each other)*
THE DEVIL IS ABROAD ON A SUNDAY MORNING!

HENRIETTE *(to her* **CHILDREN**, *but pointedly to* **FLORINA**)
TAKE A KNEE, TAKE A KNEE,
FOR THOSE LESS FORTUNATE THAN OURSELVES!

CHILDREN
YES, MAMA.

HENRIETTE
TAKE A KNEE, TAKE A KNEE AND BOW YOUR HEAD ...
THE DEVIL NEVER RESTS TILL THE DEVIL IS SURE YOU'RE
DEAD!

Light and polite.

FLORINA Henriette!

HENRIETTE Florina! I thought you'd be pleased to hear that
Mistress Hanneke seemed a little better this morning.

FLORINA You've been to visit?

HENRIETTE Yes, I thought I'd take her some of our fresh bread.

FLORINA How thoughtful of you... *(Aside to* **JOHAN**) If she ever
needs a weapon!

They smirk to each other.

HENRIETTE *(to* **FATHER ABRAM**) Has the new teacher arrived
yet, Father Abram?

FR ABRAM Not yet, Henriette, but I am expecting him at church
this morning! *(Moving on)* Now, are we ready to rehearse
our hymn, children? We want it to be perfect!

The **CHILDREN** *get into place.*

Good! Face the front and remember those D's!

CHILDREN *(sung badly)*
SHALL WE GATHER AT THE RIVER,
WHERE BRIGHT ANGEL FEET HAVE TROD;
WITH ITS CRYSTAL TIDE FOREVER
FLOWING BY THE THRONE OF GOD?

FR ABRAM And the congregation to join in here, please...

ALL *(the* **ADULTS** *join in, but they are distracted by the news of the arrival)*
YES WE'LL GATHER AT THE RIVER,
THE BEAUTIFUL, THE BEAUTIFUL RIVER;
GATHER WITH THE SAINTS BY THE RIVER
THAT FLOWS BY THE THRONE OF—!

KLAUS Does anyone know this newcomer's name?

FR ABRAM I believe it's a Mr Crane.

The questions gradually become more intense.

JOHAN Where's he come from?

FR ABRAM I think he was sent. From Connecticut.

The **TENANT FARMERS** *are collectively horrified.*

JOHAN Connecticut?! I don't like it!

FLORINA How long is he staying?

FR ABRAM *(defensive)* I don't know, Herr Van Ripper dealt with the arrangements.

FR ABRAM *goes back to the choir.*

KLAUS I don't like the idea of some stranger coming to our town!

JOHAN Why can't Father Abram teach the children?

FLORINA Father Abram? Did you just hear the choir? He has *no* control over the children.

HENRIETTE No control over *your* children.

FLORINA At least my children can sing in tune!

HENRIETTE My children are in tune with each other!

FR ABRAM *(interrupting)*
SETTLE DOWN, SETTLE DOWN, PLEASE!

JOHAN

FLORINA!

KLAUS

HENRIETTE!

Both men retrieve their wives and sit them down.

FR ABRAM

THANK YOU.

HAVE A CARE, HAVE A CARE ...

THE DEVIL NEVER RESTS ON THE TONGUES OF WOMEN.

Both women stand again as if to thump him.

HENRIETTE How dare you!

FLORINA Ooo, you...!

FR ABRAM

WHAT I MEAN IS ...

HERE WE ARE, HERE WE ARE,

WE'LL EXTEND OUR HAND IN A CHRISTIAN WELCOME

AND LET HIM IN. WON'T WE? *WON'T WE?*

ADULTS *(not won over)*

LET HIM IN, LET HIM IN, DO YOU THINK WE SHOULD?

THE DEVIL NEVER RESTS, AND THE DEVIL NEVER DID NO

GOOD!

DRIKA *and* **MARKUS** *enter* – **MARKUS** *is habitually drunk/hungover.*

HENRIETTE *(referring to* **MARKUS***)* Heaven preserve us!

MARKUS *opens his mouth to tell the news as* **DRIKA** *interrupts with her gossip.*

DRIKA

MOVE ALONG, MOVE ALONG!

FLORINA

DRIKA!

DRIKA
DID HE TELL YOU?

JOHAN
WHO?

FLORINA
WHAT?

DRIKA
MARKUS!
COULD BE WRONG, COULD BE WRONG, BUT
THE DEVIL NEVER RESTS EVEN WHEN HE'S DRINKING ...

MARKUS *belches.*

MARKUS
'SCUSE ME.

DRIKA
VAN RIPPER TOLD HIM –

MARKUS
HE ARRIVED IN TOWN ON A THIN BLACK MARE ONLY
     YESTERDAY ...

DRIKA Late last night, apparently!
MORE THAN THAT, MORE THAN THAT NO ONE CAN SAY ...
BUT THE DEVIL NEVER RESTS,

ALL
THE DEVIL NEVER RESTS;

DRIKA
AND THE DEVIL IS NEVER EVER FAR AWAY
Herr Van Fleet is probably bringing him to church as we
speak.

MARKUS The old devil bringing in the new!

JOHAN What are you talking about?

MARKUS That blasted landlord wanted two thirds of my barley
this month!

KLAUS It has been a good harvest, Markus...

MARKUS For *you* maybe! I haven't grown nearly as much as you two.

JOHAN You might've if you hadn't been drunk all the time...

MARKUS *(ignoring JOHAN)* Well he's still a bastard and should only have taken half!

There is horror at this language in church.

FR ABRAM Please, let's not speak ill of our patron Herr Van Fleet... Please, please back to our hymn! Everybody...

ALL
YES WE'LL GATHER AT THE RIVER,
THE BEAUTIFUL, THE BEAUTIFUL RIVER;
GATHER WITH THE SAINTS BY THE RIVER
THAT FLOWS BY THE THRONE OF –

ESPEN *(on lookout)* Van Fleet is here!

The Van Fleet family enters: BALTUS VAN FLEET (fifty plus) is pushed in a wheelchair by VAN RIPPER. Despite his poor health and advanced years BALTUS is a powerful man with a provoking attitude. His wife LISBETH VAN FLEET (forty) is beautiful and demure, and the congregation respect this powerful couple. KATRINA VAN FLEET (eighteen), their only child, takes after her mother in looks and temperament whilst her fiancé, BROM VAN BRUNT, is a strong 'heart and soul of the land' outside type. BROM's sister, EVA VAN BRUNT (fifteen) and VAN RIPPER's Clerk, WILLEM (eighteen) follow.

VAN RIPPER
COMING THROUGH, COMING THROUGH!

BALTUS
VAN RIPPER!

TENANT FARMERS
VAN FLEET.

BALTUS
THIS MAN ...

VAN RIPPER
AH YES?

BALTUS *(to* **VAN RIPPER***)*
WHERE IS HE?!

VAN RIPPER
NOT A CLUE, NOT A CLUE,

BALTUS
CHRIST! THE DEVIL NEVER RESTS IN SLEEPY HOLLOW!

ALL
THE DEVIL NEVER RESTS IN SLEEPY HOLLOW!

ALL, VARIOUSLY

SOMEONE NEW, SOMEONE NEW!	SHALL WE GATHER AT THE RIVER
WHERE'S HE COME FROM?	WHERE BRIGHT ANGEL FEET
WHO IS HE?	HAVE TROD?
NOT A CLUE NOT A CLUE, BUT	WITH ITS CRYSTAL TIDE FOREVER
THE DEVIL NEVER RESTS IN SLEEPY HOLLOW	FLOWING BY THE THRONE OF...

All

ESPEN *(who has been keeping lookout at the church door)* I think I see him coming!

ALL

CHANGE IS ON THE WAY, THAT MUCH IS CLEAR:
BUT IF THE DEVIL NEVER, DEVIL NEVER, DEVIL NEVER RESTS,
IS THE DEVIL HERE?

The congregation are standing with their hymn books open when **ICHABOD CRANE** *(twenty two) opens the door.*

ICHABOD
GOOD DAY. MY NAME IS ICHABOD CRANE.

There is silence as they stare.

FATHER ABRAM *dutifully steps forward.*

FR ABRAM A warm welcome to our humble little town, Mr Crane. We have been eagerly awaiting your arrival and are overjoyed to extend to you a very warm-hearted Christian welcome. Please, come, I have saved a seat for you at the front!

ICHABOD If it's all the same with you I'd rather stay at the back.

The **TENANT FARMERS** *gasp.*

FR ABRAM *(unsure)* Oh? Yes. Certainly. If you're sure...

BALTUS *(he groans, interrupting)* You heard him, Father Abram! – He wants to stand at the back. Now get on with it!

FR ABRAM Yes, of course.

FATHER ABRAM *walks swiftly to the choir and raises his arms to conduct.*

FR ABRAM Right...our hymn, children.

[MUSIC NO. 3b: "TRANSITION – SHALL WE GATHER AT THE RIVER"]

During the transition the company turn the scene to outside the church whilst singing. The congregation are saying goodbye to **FATHER ABRAM** – *shaking hands as they leave.*

ALL

SHALL WE GATHER AT THE RIVER
WHERE BRIGHT ANGEL FEET HAVE TROD?
WITH ITS CRYSTAL TIDE FOREVER,
FLOWING BY THE THRONE OF GOD?

IMOGEN & CHORUS

AND SO

AND SO
IT HAD BEGUN!

Outside the Church

The congregation disperses through the scene.

BALTUS *is not a well man and frequently coughs and splutters. Despite his abrupt manner he is not entirely unlikeable.*

BALTUS *(bluntly)* Father Abram, make the sermon shorter next week.

FR ABRAM *(bows his head apologetically)* Yes, Herr Van Fleet.

BALTUS *(turning to* **ICHABOD***)* Crane! So, you're the new teacher, are you? This is my wife, Lisbeth, and I believe you met Herr Van Ripper when you arrived last night. He'll show you everything you need in the town.

ICHABOD Thank you.

BALTUS You'll have dinner at ours tonight.

LISBETH Baltus, are you sure?

BALTUS *(hushing her)* Yes, of course!

ICHABOD If it's not inconvenient...

BALTUS *(abruptly)* Katrina?

KATRINA *(suddenly appearing)* I'm here, father!

KATRINA *reassuringly puts her hand on her* **FATHER**'s *shoulder.*

BALTUS *(tenderly and with pride he presents her to* **ICHABOD***)* This is my daughter, Katrina. *(Aside to* **KATRINA***)* You may stay and make your acquaintance with the new school teacher, but then get yourself safely home. Do you understand?

KATRINA *(understanding he is ill and wants to get home)* Of course, father, Brom will escort me to the house.

BALTUS Very well. Lisbeth, take me on!

LISBETH *wheels* BALTUS *off.*

RIPPER Ah! Brom! *(Beckons him over)* This is Brom Van Brunt, he is the steward on the Van Fleet estate. Gentlemen, if you'll excuse me. *(He goes to speak to* WILLEM*)*

BROM *and* ICHABOD *acknowledge their obvious differences -* BROM *has had a life of physical outside work and* ICHABOD *has had a life of inside study.*

BROM Teacher.

ICHABOD Please, call me Ichabod.

BROM *(finds the name hilarious)* Ichabod!

He slaps ICHABOD *on the back, in jest, yet almost winding him with his strength. Once* ICHABOD *recovers he looks at* BROM *incredulously.* BROM *is aware of his faux pas and changes the subject by taking* KATRINA*'s hand.*

Did you meet, Katrina? *(He puts his arm around her making it clear to* ICHABOD *that she is his)* We're to be wed.

ICHABOD Congratulations.

KATRINA Thank you.

ICHABOD When's the wedding?

BROM *(defensive. It's a sore point)* As soon as the good Lord allows, Mr Crane!

KATRINA It was meant to be last week, but father has been so ill that we decided to delay it.

BROM Just for a month or two while he gets better.

KATRINA *and* BROM *force a smile at each other.*

ICHABOD *(jovially)* Well, I look forward to hearing wedding bells soon!

KATRINA Yes… *(Changing the subject)* Perhaps Brom and I could show you around Sleepy Hollow this afternoon?

ICHABOD That would be perfect.

BROM I can't today.

KATRINA *(noticeably disappointed, aside to* **BROM***)* Why? I thought you were coming back to the house?

BROM *(taking* **KATRINA** *aside)* I have to go down to the lower farm on business. You don't mind, do you? *(She can't object)* I won't be long, I promise. I'll be back for dinner. *(He kisses her on the cheek and then says to both of them)* I'll see you two later...

He leaves. **ICHABOD** *and* **KATRINA** *are now awkwardly left alone together.*

KATRINA *(to* **ICHABOD***)* Perhaps some other time then...

ICHABOD Do you need escorting home?

KATRINA No, not at all, I've lived here all my life. We all have.

ICHABOD And what a beautiful place to live! I wonder why more people don't come here?

KATRINA The river and hills make it very hard for people to come or leave Sleepy Hollow.

ICHABOD Well, it certainly was a difficult ride!

KATRINA Do you know how to get to us this evening?

ICHABOD Herr Van Ripper gave me a map!

He gets the map from his pocket.

KATRINA *(looking at the map)* Yes... If you take this path from the Church along the river, you'll get to a fork in the road. Continue to the left and then you'll see the house ahead of you. Just here. *(She points on the map)*

ICHABOD And this road to the right? What's this?

KATRINA That's the Hollow Wood. But I wouldn't go there, Mr Crane.

ICHABOD Thieves?

KATRINA *(matter of fact)* No, it's haunted.

ICHABOD Haunted?

He smirks.

[MUSIC NO. 3c: "TRANSITION – INTO VAN FLEET'S"]

KATRINA And this cross here, in the centre. *(She points at the map)* That's the White Oak. It's the oldest in the hollow and it's where The Headless Horseman was buried.

ICHABOD *(incredulously)* The Headless Horseman?

VAN RIPPER *returns.*

RIPPER Ah, Miss Katrina is filling you in on local legend, Mr Crane.

ICHABOD More a case of local superstitions, I think...

KATRINA *(slightly affronted)* I had best be getting home. Till tonight, Mr Crane.

They watch **KATRINA** *leave.*

The chorus shift the scene around **ICHABOD** *as they sing:*
THE RIVER SINGS ITS GRACEFUL AIR,
THE EVENING LIGHT NOW HAS ITS LULLABY.
THE HOLLOW DARKENS BY THE HOUR
FOREVER WATCHING WITH A STEADY EYE ...

We see **THE INDIAN GIRL** *as the scene changes.*

The Van Fleet House – One

BALTUS, LISBETH, ICHABOD and KATRINA have finished dinner at the VAN FLEET household – wine has been drunk – candles burning low. The debate is jovial yet heated.

ICHABOD ... *(In the middle of conversation)* I was very lucky to have such an informative, progressive education and I truly believe knowledge is everything, it's what saves lives, feeds industry and stops communities being controlled by religion or silly superstitions.

LISBETH *(intake of breath)* I'm not sure Father Abram will agree!

ICHABOD *(resolutely)* There are still many things we can't explain, but it's only a matter of time. Knowledge builds knowledge.

BALTUS Well, perhaps you are right, science does seem to be the modern way of thinking...but here, all the children really need to learn is how to farm.

ICHABOD Surely, they need to know about the world!

BALTUS You can teach them what you want, Crane, but at the end of the day they'll be working the land.

ICHABOD I can't accept that.

BALTUS How else is a man to survive in an isolated rural community like Sleepy Hollow?

ICHABOD Perhaps, but what of the women in the town? Katrina, for example? Will she plough the fields and milk the cows?

BALTUS *(firmly)* No... She will provide a son to take over the estate.

ICHABOD *(incredulously)* I can't believe what I'm hearing?! Things are changing! *(Taking the plunge into a controversial matter)* I fully intend that my lessons will be as equally as informative for girls as they are for boys.

BALTUS *(laughing as he's heard it all before)* Old Hanneke thought the same.

ICHABOD *(unable to let it go)* Well, she's right! I'm very much looking forward to building on the foundations Mistress Hanneke made! *(Bringing* **KATRINA** *into the debate)* What do you think, Katrina? *(She looks at him, startled)*

KATRINA I'm sorry?

ICHABOD What do you think of all this?

There is a pause.

BALTUS Katrina is a good girl...she knows how it is.

KATRINA *(faltering)* I think...education is important, but I think it's foolish to discard what we don't understand simply because we don't understand it.

ICHABOD *(agreeing)* Yes, there are still many things that haven't been explained or discovered, *(pursuing his cause)* but some things, like spirits or ghosts or *God,* will never be explained. Because they simply don't exist!

There is silence. The family clearly believe in ghosts and God.

BALTUS Our community will disagree with you.

ICHABOD *(gently mocking)* Ah yes, the 'haunted' Hollow Wood. Katrina mentioned it earlier, something about a tree marking a grave... The Headless Horseman!

BALTUS *(sternly)* I wouldn't make fun of it, Mr Crane.

ICHABOD *is aware he has gone too far.*

[MUSIC NO. 4: "THE TALE OF THE HEADLESS HORSEMAN"]

It strikes me that you should learn *our* ways first, and then see if there is a need for *your* ways of educating. The Horseman isn't just a story, it's part of our history.

AT THE CENTRE OF THE HOLLOW WOOD,
THERE STANDS A MIGHTY TREE.
THEY SAY THAT HE IS BURIED THERE;
HIS BODY ROTS, BUT HIS SPIRIT RIDES, FREE.

THEY SAY HE WAS AN ARMY MAN,
WHO SLEW SOME INDIAN CHILD
THEN LOST HIS HEAD ON HOLLOW SOIL,
NO RECOMPENSE FOR BLOODY TOIL;
SO HE RIDES!

YOU HEAR HIM AS THE SUN GOES DOWN!
A THUNDER IN THE GLOOM.

NO FENCE OR GATE CAN BAR HIS WAY,
YOU DREAD THE NIGHT AND RUE THE DAY
THAT HE RIDES!

THE FLANKS OF HIS STEED ARE ALL SPECKLED WITH SWEAT,
ITS EYES ARE DILATED IN PAIN,
AS HE PUSHES THE ANIMAL *ON! FASTER YET!*
A SPEED NO ORDINARY BEAST COULD SUSTAIN.

POUNDING THE EARTH WHERE HIS OWN BLOOD WAS SHED,
NOT SLOWING, NOT STOPPING FOR BREATH;
HE SEEKS THE REMAINS OF HIS SEVERED HEAD!
IF YOU SEE HIM,
WHEN YOU SEE HIM,
MUTTER YOUR PRAYERS IN THE DARKNESS,
IT CAN MEAN ONLY
DEATH!

He goes into a coughing fit and is clearly in pain.
LISBETH *fetches some water. During the commotion*
KATRINA *and* **ICHABOD** *continue the conversation.*

KATRINA *(aside to* **ICHABOD***)* Ever since the Dutch settlers came here there have been strange sightings in the Hollow Wood... ghosts of soldiers, screaming women, children covered in blood...

ICHABOD *(dismissively)* Ah, the malevolent spirits seeking justice...

KATRINA There is *one* different from the rest. We think of her as being a guardian of the land...

ICHABOD Let me guess, the Indian child killed by the Horseman.

KATRINA Yes. The black-eyed girl is a reminder of the people who were here before us.

ICHABOD What makes you think she's so different?

A sudden furious knocking breaks the atmosphere.

BALTUS *(calling)* Come in! Come in!

BROM *(entering)* Sorry I'm late. I had to see to the cattle on the top field.

BALTUS Katrina, get Crane's hat and coat. (**KATRINA** *does so*) Lisbeth, take me on!

ICHABOD *(surprised by the abrupt end to the evening)* Thank you for your hospitality.

LISBETH Goodbye, Mr Crane.

> **LISBETH** *wheels* **BALTUS** *out.*

> **BROM** *starts helping himself to the food on the table, biting off meat from a drumstick.* **KATRINA** *returns with* **ICHABOD**'s *hat and coat.*

BROM Evening, teacher. Good dinner?

ICHABOD Yes. *(Mocking)* Herr Van Fleet was telling me about the spirits *haunting* the Hollow Wood.

> **BROM** *is not amused by his mocking.*

BROM Well? What of them?

ICHABOD You can't possibly believe –

BROM *(challenging)* Why don't you ride up to the Hollow Wood at dusk and tell us what you see.

KATRINA *(gently)* Brom...

ICHABOD I accept that sometimes the evening light can play tricks with the eyes ...but whatever you saw wasn't a "ghost".

BROM What do you mean by that?

KATRINA *(gently imploring)* Brom, please.

ICHABOD There has to be a more tangible explanation.

BROM *(confrontational)* Such as?

ICHABOD It could be any number of things...the light, shadows, indulging at the local inn –

BROM Are you saying I'm a drunk?

ICHABOD Not at all. I'm merely saying you've been deceived in some way.

LISBETH *appears back at the door to fetch* BROM *to* VAN FLEET.

LISBETH Brom, he needs you in the study.

BROM *(to* ICHABOD*)* Goodnight, Mr Crane.

BROM *leaves with* LISBETH, *continuing to munch on the drumstick.* KATRINA *shows* ICHABOD *out alone.*

[MUSIC NO. 4b: "TRANSITION - HOMEWARD"]

KATRINA Please forgive them. They're not used to being challenged.

ICHABOD *(gently)* How can anyone believe that there is a wood full of spirits?

KATRINA It's as you said, there are many things we can't explain, *(elaborating on his point)* but just because we can't explain them, it doesn't mean they are not there. Goodnight, Mr Crane.

CHORUS *transition, with* IMOGEN *and* JOSHUA *looking on.*

CHORUS

SMALL TOWN GREAT SHAME
ICHABOD CRANE TRAVELLED HOMEWARD
AND WHEN THE MORNING CAME ...

The Schoolroom

[MUSIC NO. 5: "POOR LITTLE TOM"]

Next morning the **CHILDREN** *are rushing to school, with an air of excitement and childish innocence.*

CHILDREN
POOR LITTLE TOM SHOULDA LEARNED HIS LETTERS,
POOR LITTLE TOM SHOULDA LEARNED TO READ;
WHEN POOR LITTLE TOM COULDN'T READ HIS BIBLE
LITTLE TOM'S MOTHER WAS CROSS INDEED.

'CAUSE POOR LITTLE TOM COULDN'T READ HIS BIBLE,
POOR LITTLE TOM COULDN'T SAY HIS PRAYERS;
LITTLE TOM'S MOTHER WAS POWERFUL ANGRY,
SHE PUSHED LITTLE TOM RIGHT DOWN THE STAIRS!

POOR LITTLE TOM SHOULDA LEARNED HIS LETTERS,
POOR LITTLE TOM SHOULDA TAKEN HEED;
OH, POOR LITTLE TOM HAD A POOR OLD ENDING
'CAUSE POOR LITTLE TOM NEVER LEARNED TO READ!

The **CHILDREN** *are in the classroom creating havoc.* **ICHABOD** *creeps in and observes. A child notices him and tugs at another, etc, till the whole class are aware of his presence.*

ISAAC Sorry, sir. We didn't know that you were there.

ICHABOD Why should you act any differently when I am here?

ISAAC I don't know, sir.

ICHABOD So, tell me what happened to Little Tom?

RUTH He died.

ABEL Mother says that when you pass the schoolhouse at night, you can still hear him stumbling over his Bible verses...

ICHABOD *(amused)* Well, I shall listen out for him! Are there any more ghost stories I should know?

They all put their hands up.

ICHABOD Oh! I see! Perhaps I should hear them another time! *(He indicates for them to put their hands down)* My name is Mr Crane.

CHILDREN Good morning, Mr Crane.

ICHABOD Before we start, perhaps it might be a good idea to see what you already know.

The **CHILDREN** *look at each other.*

What was the last thing you were reading with Mistress Hanneke?

ESTHER Sir, we were learning lesson seventeen on page twenty five.

ICHABOD And can anyone tell me what happened in lesson seventeen?

[MUSIC NO. 6: "THE NEW ENGLAND PRIMER"]

CHILDREN *(all together, expressionless)*
CHARLES, WILL YOU WALK?
NO, IT IS TOO DIRTY.
WHEN YOU ARE OLDER YOU SHALL HAVE TROUSERS
AND A PAIR OF LITTLE BOOTS
AND THEN YOU SHALL GO IN THE DIRT

ICHABOD I don't think I know that one...

ROSA Please, sir, there's more.

ICHABOD There is?

CHILDREN *(all together, expressionless)*
CHARLES, HERE IS MARY
COME FROM THE FAIR;
WHAT HAS SHE BROUGHT?
SHE HAS BROUGHT CHARLES
A GUN AND A SWORD
AND A HAMMER
AND SOME CAKE.

ICHABOD *is quietly horrified by this archaic format and without wanting to offend stops the class.*

ICHABOD   I see...right, thank you, that's enough of that. *(Tentatively)* Um...shall we move on to some writing? How have you been practicing your letters?

ISAAC *puts his hand up.*

Yes, what's your name?

ISAAC Isaac, sir. Mistress Hanneke would usually have us copy out a passage from our primers.

ICHABOD Very well, turn to the last page you were on, and pick up from there. You have five minutes.

ICHABOD *walks to the back of the class.*

CHILDREN *(singing sweetly while they write)*
KEEP THY TONGUE FROM ILL AND THY LIPS FROM GUILE
LET THY WORDS BE TRUE TO THY HEART ...

The music suddenly changes and it is spooky as hell.
FOR THE TIME WILL COME WHEN WE ALL WILL BE LAID IN
    THE DUST

ICHABOD *(reading the last sentence over a shoulder)* Good grief, what text is this?

He takes the book from the desk.

MARTHA The New England Primer.

ICHABOD That book is nearly fifty years old! Have you read nothing of Benjamin Franklin? Amelia Simpson?

The CHILDREN *look blank.*

What about arithmetic?

CHILDREN
ONE TIMES ONE IS ONE
ONE TIMES TWO IS TWO
ONE TIMES THREE IS ...

ICHABOD Anything a little more advanced...?

CHILDREN
SIX TIMES ONE IS SIX
SIX TIMES TWO IS TWELVE
SIX TIMES THREE IS EIGHTEEN
SIX TIMES FOUR IS TWENTY FOUR

ICHABOD Stop! Stop! That's enough!

Pause.

What do you know about science?

The CHILDREN *look vacant.*

Has anyone heard of Galileo? *(Pause)* Hypatia? Hildegard?
Da Vinci...?

(pause) Anybody?

CHILDREN No, Mr Crane.

**[*MUSIC NO. 7 : "WE USED TO THINK THE EARTH
WAS FLAT"*]**

ICHABOD Surely you have questions about the world? Why
things happen the way they do? You. *(he points at a child)*
What's your name?

JAKOB Jakob, sir.

ICHABOD Why do we sweat on a hot day?

JAKOB Don't know...

ICHABOD Why does our breath steam on a cold day? How are
clouds formed? Why does the earth move around the sun?

JAKOB Why do we care?

ICHABOD Why do we care? Why *do* we care?
WE USED TO THINK THE EARTH WAS FLAT.
WE USED TO THINK THAT THAT WAS HOW IT WAS CREATED;
THAT AT THE EDGE ONLY OBLIVION AWAITED ...
WE USED TO THINK THE EARTH WAS FLAT.

BUT THEN WE LEARNED TO LOOK AROUND,
WE MAPPED OUR JOURNEYS THROUGH THE MOUNTAINS
   'CROSS THE OCEANS
WE DID AWAY WITH ALL THOSE RUDIMENTARY NOTIONS
BECAUSE WE LEARNED TO LOOK AROUND ...

WE FOUND OUR PLACE AMONG THE STARS
WE DREW OUR DIAGRAMS AND MADE OUR OBSERVATIONS
WE NAMED THE PLANETS AND THEIR MOONS AND
   CONSTELLATIONS
WE FOUND OUR PLACE AMONG THE STARS!

FOR EVERY HOW AND WHY AND WHERE
THERE IS AN ANSWER WAITING THERE IN THE WORLD;
BENEATH EACH ROCK, BENEATH EACH STONE
BENEATH EACH MYSTERY AND UNKNOWN
THERE IS A UNIVERSAL TRUTH
THAT WE ARE WAITING TO BE SHOWN!

AND EVERY SINGLE ONE OF YOU
HAS THE CAPACITY TO THINK AND FEEL AND QUESTION
I ONLY ASK THAT YOU ARE OPEN TO SUGGESTION
WE USED TO THINK THE EARTH WAS FLAT ...

(spoken) Close your primers, children. Open a blank page...

Market Day

[MUSIC NO. 8: "THE LIFE WE LIVE"]

Transition: Street scene – the comings and goings of the village – barter, trade, fetching and carrying – the hard work of daily life. ICHABOD *is walking through the town.*

BROM

THERE'S A BROAD SKY,
AND A HOT SUN SHINING.
IT'S A PLEASING LAND,
BUT A HARD ONE TOO.

MEN

IT'S EARTH TO HAND AND HAND TO MOUTH
FROM DAWN TO DUSK, FROM NORTH TO SOUTH.
YOU SOW, YOU REAP, YOU SOW AGAIN;
THIS IS NO LIFE FOR IDLE MEN!

BROM

BUT IT'S BEEN LIKE THIS SINCE HISTORY BEGAN:
YOU LIVE THE LIFE YOU LIVE, AS BEST YOU CAN.

VAN RIPPER *and* **BALTUS** *are talking and call over* **BROM**.

BALTUS How are the upper farms doing?

BROM Some better than others. Barley is good this year.

BALTUS Percentages?

RIPPER Based on their yield I should say two thirds.

HENRIETTE, FLORINA, DRIKA, EVA AND ESTHER

IT'S A LONG DAY
AND IT'S ALL SPENT WORKING.
IT'S A PLEASING LAND,
BUT THERE'S MUCH TO DO.
IT'S EARTH TO HAND AND HAND TO PLATE
YOU FEED ANOTHER MAN'S ESTATE.

HUSBANDS (**JOHAN, MARKUS** *and* **KLAUS** *put out their produce for inspection*)
YOU SOW, YOU REAP; YOU PAY YOUR DUES,
THERE IS NO OTHER LIFE TO CHOOSE,
BUT YOU WONDER IF THERE'S SOMETHING BETTER THAN
JUST TO LIVE THE LIFE YOU LIVE, AS BEST YOU CAN.

*BALTUS, VAN RIPPER and BROM inspect the produce of
KLAUS, HENRIETTE, JOHAN and FLORINA.*

DRIKA (*hushed to* **MARKUS**) Is that all you've got? Oh lord!
He'll be expecting more than that...

*DRIKA has an idea and puts a bunch of carrots into
the bag and closes it. BALTUS arrives at DRIKA and
MARKUS's produce.*

BALTUS (*looking at the bag*) What's in there?

DRIKA (*nervously*) Barley?

*BALTUS indicates to bring the bag over and weigh it.
VAN RIPPER does so. As it hangs from the weighing scale
BALTUS opens up the bag to look in it. He pulls out the
carrots.*

BALTUS (*threateningly*) Did you really think you could cheat
me out of my share with a few carrots?!

*He throws the carrots at DRIKA's feet and she defends
herself as if they might strike her.*

Now get what's due to me before the sun goes down. I *know*
you're good for it! Take me on!

*The women get down on the floor to pick up the carrots.
ICHABOD helps.*

ICHABOD Are you alright?

DRIKA Oh! I've had worse! But you can't blame him. He's got
a family to feed an all...

ICHABOD How does it work?

DRIKA Well... Van Fleet provides the land –

HENRIETTE And seeds –

FLORINA And tools –

DRIKA And in return we give Herr Van Fleet two thirds of everything we grow.

ICHABOD *(amazed)* Two thirds?!

MARKUS *(agreeing with* **ICHABOD**'s *sentiment)* If it's a good harvest – half if it's not.

ICHABOD So much! I wonder you don't buy the land and keep the profits yourself! Thanks for the carrots!

   ICHABOD *pays and leaves.*

   The **TENANT FARMERS** *look out to the front and think about what* **ICHABOD** *has just said.*

TENANT FARMERS
   IT'S A FAIR POINT
   THAT WE'D NOT CONSIDERED
   IT'S A PLEASING LAND,
   THAT WE DO NOT OWN!
   IT'S EARTH TO HAND, AND HAND TO CAP,
   WE'RE DONE WITH THE WRETCHED LANDLORD'S CRAP
   WE SOW WE REAP, WE GIVE GIVE GIVE;
   IS THERE ANOTHER LIFE TO LIVE?
   WE MUST BE PART OF SOME ETERNAL PLAN ...
   EVERY WOMAN, EVERY CHILD AND EVERY SIMPLE WORKING
      MAN!
   SO IT'S HAND TO HEART WITH HEAD HELD HIGH,
   AS DECENT FOLK WE CAN BUT TRY
   TO LIVE THE LIFE WE LIVE AS BEST WE CAN!
   AS BEST WE CAN!
   AS BEST WE CAN!

Eva and Brom's House

Since their mother's death a year ago EVA *(sixteen) has been housekeeper to her brother* BROM. ICHABOD *has come to visit and is talking to* EVA *in the kitchen when* KATRINA *arrives.*

KATRINA *(calling as she enters)* Hello? Eva?

She enters to find ICHABOD *laughing with* EVA.

ICHABOD Miss Katrina.

EVA Mr Crane has brought me a book.

KATRINA How kind.

ICHABOD Father Abram told me how Miss Eva had to stop her schooling after her mother passed away.

EVA We were just talking about New York City.

ICHABOD *(to* EVA*)* I think you would like it there very much. I know I did.

EVA I don't think there's any chance of me ever going.

ICHABOD Why not?

EVA Perhaps...one day.

Pause.

ICHABOD *(aware of intruding on their time together)* Please forgive me! I should leave you two to talk.

KATRINA Oh, no...please... I didn't mean to cut short your stay...

ICHABOD I expect you'll have more fun without me here. Good luck with the reading, Miss Eva. Goodbye.

He leaves hastily, to KATRINA*'s obvious disappointment.* EVA *observes* KATRINA*'s interest in* ICHABOD. KATRINA *becomes uncomfortable under* EVA*'s scrutinising look.*

KATRINA What?

EVA *(knowingly)* Nothing.

KATRINA *(picking up the book)* It was thoughtful of him to bring you this.

EVA *(pointedly)* Yes, but I think it was best he left before Brom got home.

KATRINA *looks confused.*

Here, help me with these, will you?

She pulls out a basket of sheets and they start folding. KATRINA *pulls out various bits of linen.*

KATRINA What's that smell?

EVA What? (EVA *takes the shirt to smell)* I've only just washed it!

KATRINA No, something else...

EVA Oh, that! I'm boiling up a pig's head for brawn...

KATRINA Well, I suppose it's something to do with leftovers.

EVA ...but I haven't got enough pots.

KATRINA I'm sure we've got some spare, if you want them.

EVA Have you?

KATRINA I'll bring them next time.

[MUSIC NO. 9: "ALL TOO SOON"]

KATRINA *picks up some socks and pairs them.*

Do you ever cook pastries? Like your mother?

EVA No, I'm terrible at it and Brom only eats savoury things like boiled beef...

KATRINA *(straight faced)* Boiled beef...

EVA I tried to make a pumpkin pie once...but even the pigs wouldn't eat it.

They burst out laughing.

WHEN DID WE GROW UP?

WHEN DID WE STOP BEING US?

WHEN DID POTS AND PANS AND PASTRIES BECOME THE
THINGS THAT WE DISCUSS?

BOTH

WHEN DID WE GROW UP?

KATRINA

WE USED TO TELL EACH OTHER STORIES,

BOTH

WE USED TO DREAM EACH OTHERS DREAMS!

NOW HERE WE ARE:

KATRINA

A WIFE TO BE,

EVA

A HOUSEKEEPER

IS IT AS SILLY AS IT SEEMS ...?

KATRINA

I REMEMBER HOW IN CHURCH YOU WOULD SING JUST A
LITTLE BIT FLAT!

EVA

ON PURPOSE!

KATRINA

IT DROVE POOR FATHER ABRAM ROUND THE TWIST!

EVA

HE HATED ME!

AND I REMEMBER HOW IN SCHOOL

YOU BOXED THE EARS OF ADAM VAN ... KANT?

KATRINA

VAN SANT?

BOTH

VAN BLATT!

EVA

WHEN HE TOLD THE CLASS THAT YOU AND HE HAD KISSED!

KATRINA Not with that breath!

EVA

AND D'YOU REMEMBER HOW WE'D RUN

KATRINA

WE WOULD RUN

BOTH

AS QUICKLY AS OUR PETTICOATS ALLOWED
GUIDED BY THE SHINING SUMMER MOON?

EVA

OH, KATRINA, WE WERE FUN!

KATRINA

WE WERE FREE, WE WERE FOOLISH,

BOTH

WE WERE LOUD!

EVA

WHEN DID WE GROW UP?
ALL TOO SOON.

They continue folding.

I REMEMBER YOU WERE SICK

KATRINA

WHAT?

EVA

IN THE STREET

KATRINA

WHEN?!

EVA

AT THE MIDSUMMER FAIR ...

KATRINA

OH YES!

TOO MUCH OF YOUR MOTHER'S DAMSON PIE!

AND D'YOU REMEMBER WHEN WE HID?

EVA

WHY?

KATRINA

IN THE WOOD

EVA

YES! WE THOUGHT THE HORSEMAN WAS THERE!

KATRINA

I WAS TERRIFIED ...

TURNED OUT IT WAS YOUR BROTHER RIDING BY!

EVA

IDIOT.

KATRINA

AND D'YOU REMEMBER HOW WE'D DANCE

EVA

WE WOULD DANCE

BOTH

AS LATE INTO THE EVENING AS WE COULD

LISTENING TO THEM PLAY THE HARVEST TUNE!

KATRINA

WE LEFT EVERYTHING TO CHANCE,

EVA

OR TO LUCK

KATRINA

WE MADE MISCHIEF

EVA

WE STILL SHOULD!

BOTH

WHEN DID WE GROW UP?
WHY SHOULD WE GROW UP?!
WHY SHOULD WE GROW UP?!
WHY SHOULD WE GROW UP?!

HEY HEY HEY-O!
HEY HEY HEY-O!

The two girls begin to play with the sheets, wrapping each other up, putting their arms through shirts, etc, and generally being stupid. **BROM** *bursts in and silences them.*

BROM *(angry)* What in God's name is going on? Prancing around in the house like this when there's work to be done? *(Pause)* Eva, have you looked at Meg recently? That foal is as likely to come tonight, and I'll need a change of clothes and a hot bloody meal. *(Slightly softer but disappointed)* Katrina... there can be none of this when we're married. *(To* **EVA***)* I'll be back by seven.

He leaves, the two girls are chastised.

EVA

AND WE SIMPLY COULDN'T KNOW THAT CHILDHOOD NEVER
    REALLY LASTS FOR LONG

KATRINA

LIKE SUNSHINE ON A WINTER'S AFTERNOON;

(spoken) I ought to go.

They embrace, and **KATRINA** *comes downstage as the kitchen dissolves away.* **IMOGEN** *is watching her.*

WHEN DID WE GROW UP?
ALL TOO SOON.

The Schoolroom – Two

[MUSIC NO. 10: "MR CRANE SAYS"]

A divided stage – in one space, ICHABOD *teaches his class.* CHILDREN *variously turn to converse with their parents, who inhabit their respective kitchens in other spaces. Scenes should dovetail one into the other, seamlessly.*

DRIKA*'s kitchen –* ESPEN *is poking a dead frog.*

DRIKA What are you doing to that dead frog?

ESPEN Bringing it back to life.

DRIKA Not in my kitchen you're not.

ESPEN I have to wait for a thunderstorm to strike these rods and stimulate its muscle.

DRIKA Stimulate its muscle? It's dead! And starting to smell. Take it outside.

ESPEN *(sudden thought)* Do you think we could try and bring a whole *person* back to life?

DRIKA Bless my soul, whatever gave you that idea?!

ESPEN
MR CRANE SAYS –

	ICHABOD
	GALVANISM
CHILDREN	
GALVANISM	
	G-A-L-V-A-N-I-S-M
G-A-L-V-A-N-I-S-M	
	THE CONTRACTION OF A
	MUSCLE
	STIMULATED BY AN
	ELECTRIC CURRENT
THE CONTRACTION OF A	
MUSCLE	

STIMULATED BY AN
ELECTRIC CURRENT

> YOU SEE, WE ARE MERELY
> A COLLECTION OF
> IMPULSES
> THAT FEED ORGANIC
> MATTER

WE ARE MERELY A
COLLECTION OF
IMPULSES
THAT FEED ORGANIC
MATTER

> QUESTIONS?

ESTHER
BUT WHAT ABOUT THE
SOUL?

> THE EXISTENCE OF THE
> SOUL IS THEREFORE
> SOMETHING

Taking over **ICHABOD**'*s*
words.
REQUIRING FURTHER
INVESTIGATION

We are now in **FLORINA**'*s kitchen.* **FLORINA** *is busy getting dinner ready and* **JOHAN** *is sitting by the fire.* **CHILDREN** *everywhere...*

FLORINA *(to* **ESTHER**) Sounds like Devil's talk! *(To* **MARTHA** *as if she's never seen her read a book in her life)* What are you doing?

MARTHA Reading. Mr Crane says we should take every opportunity to further ourselves.

FLORINA Not at dinner you don't! Jakob, wash your face; Abel, close the door; Ruth, get the napkins. Johan...do... *(exasperated)* something!

JOHAN You heard your mother.

FLORINA Jacob, what is with you and candles? You'll burn the house down!

JAKOB I'm making a hot air balloon. How far do you think it will go, father?

JOHAN Umm... What's a hot air balloon?

JAKOB *(as if to say it's obvious)* It's a *balloon* filled with *hot air.*

RUTH
MR CRANE SAYS

ICHABOD
IF THE TEMPERATURE INSIDE THE BAG IS HIGHER THAN THE
TEMPERATURE OUTSIDE THE BAG
THE BAG INFLATES AND THEN BEGINS TO RISE

CHILDREN
IF THE TEMPERATURE INSIDE THE BAG
IS HIGHER THAN THE TEMPERATURE OUTSIDE THE BAG
THE BAG INFLATES AND THEN BEGINS TO RISE

ICHABOD
THERE MAY WELL COME A TIME WE HARNESS THIS REACTION
AND EMPLOY THIS NEW PHENOMENON TO LEAVE THE EARTH
BEHIND ...

MARTHA Where could we go?

ICHABOD Where would you like to go?

Back to **FLORINA***'s kitchen.* **MARTHA** *is standing in the door with a suitcase.*

MARTHA Can I go to Egypt?

FLORINA Yes. When you've finished your chores.

The **CHILDREN** *laugh at their mother.*

FLORINA/JOHAN What?

ABEL Egypt is thousands of miles away!

JOHAN Well then you can't go, can you?

MARTHA But I want to see a pyramid!

FLORINA There's a pile of laundry needs seeing to first... *(Aside to* **JOHAN***)* What's a pyramid?

JOHAN Don't ask me – I'm still trying to understand the hot air balloon!

MARTHA

MR CRANE SAYS

ICHABOD

IN THE VALLEY OF THE PHARAOHS
STANDING THREE HUNDRED CUBITS TALL
IS THE GREATEST FEAT OF HUMAN ENGINEERING EVER SEEN
    UPON THE EARTH!

CHILDREN What is it? / How long's it been there? / Can we go?

ICHABOD

ITS IN THE VALLEY OF THE PHARAOHS, IN EGYPT
IT WAS BUILT OVER FOUR THOUSAND YEARS AGO!

Snap into **DRIKA** *and* **MARKUS***'s kitchen.*

ROSA

THAT'S AT LEAST TWO THOUSAND YEARS BEFORE THE BIBLE
    OR THE SO-CALLED VIRGIN BIRTH!

MARKUS What did you say?

ESPEN Why is grass green, father?

MARKUS Because it is.

ROSA How are rainbows made?

MARKUS Something to do with...rain. And...bows.

ESPEN What about snow and ice?

MARKUS Look, all I know is that God made Heaven and Earth in seven days.

REBEKAH Seven days?! *(Pause)* You don't really think *that's* true, do you?

MARKUS Erm...well...he rested on the Sunday.

REBEKAH
MR CRANE SAYS –

ICHABOD
WE LIVE IN AN AGE OF

CHILDREN
ENLIGHTENMENT!
OF SCIENCE AND PROGRESS AND FACT
WITHOUT PROOF THE ORIGINS OF LIFE REMAIN UNKNOWN

ICHABOD
AND THESE STORIES ARE ... WELL, JUST THAT ...

ANNA But what about faith?

ICHABOD Faith is not something I can teach because it requires us to believe without asking questions.

The class all look at **ICHABOD** *because of this.*

HENRIETTE's *house – she is chasing* **ANNA** *with a dress.*

HENRIETTE Anna, you get here right now!!

ANNA I hate you! I won't do it! You can't make me!

HENRIETTE Oh yes I can! Now put this dress on!

ANNA No!

HENRIETTE Yes!

ANNA No!

HENRIETTE What's got into you?

KLAUS *(coming in)* We'll be late for church...

ANNA I'm not going!

HENRIETTE For Heaven's sake why?!

ANNA I'm not going because... I don't believe in God!!!

HENRIETTE *reacts as an earth shattering chord is played. The scene changes again and suddenly all the parents are clamouring around* **FR ABRAM**.

PARENTS

MR CRANE SAYS –

WE HAVE NO SOULS!
HE CAN BRING PEOPLE BACK TO LIFE!
WHAT IS HE, JESUS?
HE SAID JESUS WAS EGYPTIAN!

MR CRANE SAYS –

THAT HE CAN FLY!
THAT HE CAN FLY IN A BALLOON;

FR ABRAM

WHAT'S A BALLOON?

PARENTS

SOME SORT OF FLOATING BAG OF EVIL!

MR CRANE SAYS
THE THINGS HE THINKS THEY SHOULD BE LEARNING
ANY MOMENT
WE'LL HEAR THE SOUND OF WITCHES BURNING!

FATHER ABRAM WON'T YOU PLEASE EXPLAIN:
THIS IS NOT HOW IT'S DONE IN SLEEPY HOLLOW, MR CRANE!

MR CRANE SAYS
THERE IS NO GOD
HE SAID THE BIBLE WAS MADE UP!
HE'S GOT THEM FISHING ROTTEN FROGS FROM OUT THE
    RIVER!

MR CRANE SAYS –
WELL, HE SAYS THINGS WE DON'T AGREE WITH
HE'S GOT THE CHILDREN ASKING QUESTIONS
THEY'RE ASKING QUESTIONS THAT WE DON'T KNOW HOW TO
    ANSWER
MR CRANE SAYS
THIS IS A ROUNDED EDUCATION;

FATHER ABRAM, WE ARE IN NEED OF YOUR SALVATION!
THE CHILDREN ARE EXPERIMENTING, ANALYZING,
    VERIFYING;
IGNORANCE WAS BLISS BUT NOW IT'S ABSOLUTELY
    TERRIFYING!

ANNA I'm not going because... I DON'T BELIEVE IN GOD!!!

FR ABRAM *(unsure)* I shall have a word. Leave it with me.

Back to **ICHABOD**'s *classroom – the end of the day.*

ICHABOD So, who can tell me what Newton's third law is?

The whole class put their hands up.

ESTHER For every action there is an equal and opposite *reaction.*

ICHABOD Therefore, if I throw this apple into the air...

RUTH Then your body exerts an equal and opposite force on the ground beneath you.

ICHABOD Excellent. That's all for today. And remember, if you have any questions, you can always ask your parents. Class dismissed.

The **CHILDREN** *leave.* **FATHER ABRAM** *is waiting to speak with* **ICHABOD**...

Father Abram Visits Mr Crane

FR ABRAM Mr Crane, I wondered if I might have a word. I only need a fraction of your time...a moment... I won't be above five minutes...

ICHABOD Very well, what can I do for you, Father Abram? *(Sympathetic)* Is it about the choir?

FR ABRAM *(confused)* No...

ICHABOD *(surprised)* Oh! What is it then?

FR ABRAM *(explaining)* It's about your teaching methods...the nature of your approach...more specifically the content.

ICHABOD How do you mean? Have the children been complaining?

FR ABRAM No...the parents.

ICHABOD About what?

FR ABRAM They say that your teachings are inappropriate for the children...

ICHABOD How so?

FR ABRAM Well...the children are asking questions...

ICHABOD That's what we want!

FR ABRAM No, I mean they are asking questions about what we believe...

ICHABOD *(pointedly)* The local legends?

FR ABRAM No...the Bible!

ICHABOD Same difference to me!

FR ABRAM *(insulted)* The Bible is absolute!

ICHABOD Talking snakes, the parting of the Red Sea... *(He leans forward)* Jonah and the Whale...even you must see how farcical it is!

FR ABRAM *is speechless.*

(reasoning) Look, I never told the children not to believe, that is not my place, I merely taught them to be inquisitive of the world around them. *(Using* FATHER ABRAM*'s words)* But just so we are clear, I think that *your* teachings are as *inappropriate* for the children as letting them believe in The Headless Horseman, The Indian Girl or any other supernatural sighting!

FR ABRAM *(pointedly)* I understand that as an *outsider* our ways may be new to you, but Mistress Hanneke never questioned our beliefs / and she...

ICHABOD And she turned out a bunch of small-minded fools who believe in ghosts!

FR ABRAM *(indignantly)* The Devil works in many ways, Mr Crane! You'd do well not to question the belief of a town or the faith of a nation.

ICHABOD *(last straw)* And you'd do as well to stop filling their heads with antiquated fairy tales and supernatural drivel! Good day, Father Abram!

FATHER ABRAM *is outraged.*

The Edge of the Wood

[MUSIC NO. 11: "BLACK-EYED SUSAN"]

The Hollow Wood, dusk. SABINE *gathers flowers and sings.* THE INDIAN GIRL *watches her from the shadows.*

SABINE

CARAWAY FOR MOTHER'S MILK,
DANDELION FOR FEVER.
FENNEL SEED FOR SUMMER'S GHOSTS,
AND ROSEMARY FOR DREAMS ...
YARROW ROOT FOR MOONTIME,
AND WILLOW FOR THE PAIN.
BUT BLACK-EYED SUSAN WILL NEVER BLOOM AGAIN!

Gradually, THE INDIAN GIRL *comes out into the open and begins to dance with* SABINE – *a conversation with no words.*

SPEAK TO ME OF COLUMBINES,
CHAMOMILE AND CHERRY!
SHOW ME WHERE THE SORREL GROWS,
TO COOL THE RAGING BLOOD ...
I AM SHE WHO LISTENS
TO THE FOREST AND THE PLAIN;
COME BLACK-EYED SUSAN, SPEAK TO ME AGAIN!

ICHABOD *has stumbled across the clearing. He sees* **SABINE**, *but he does not see* **THE INDIAN GIRL.**

DON'T YOU THINK, SIR, SHE'S THE PRETTIEST THING YOU'VE
    EVER SEEN?

ICHABOD

I SEE NO ONE, MADAM ...

SABINE

LOOK AT HER DANCE, SIR
AN EVENING SHADOW AMIDST THE GREEN ...

ICHABOD

THERE IS NO ONE THERE!!

SABINE

OH SHE WATCHES AND WAITS, SIR
AS SHE HAS DONE FOR YEARS
BUT SOON, I FEAR THAT SHE WILL SCREAM!

ICHABOD

MADAM - THERE IS NO ONE HERE!

SABINE and **THE INDIAN GIRL** *begin to dance again – reckless, beautiful.* **ICHABOD** *looks on, utterly confused.*

SABINE

CARAWAY FOR MOTHER'S MILK,
DANDELION FOR FEVER!
FIREFLIES AND SHOOTING STARS,
AND VOICES IN THE DARK!
I AM SHE WHO LISTENS
TO THE HOLLOW'S MAD REFRAIN;
COME, BLACK-EYED SUSAN ...

The **THE INDIAN GIRL** *disappears, and* **SABINE** *turns to* **ICHABOD** *and grabs his hand. We hear a pounding of hooves in the distance.*

(whispered, intense) CAN YOU HEAR IT, MR CRANE?!

She disappears into the Wood.

Snap Transition

VAN RIPPER*'s office –* **ICHABOD** *tells* **VAN RIPPER** *of his meeting with* **SABINE.**

VAN RIPPER And what did you hear?

ICHABOD I heard nothing...

VAN RIPPER *gives* **WILLEM** *a knowing look.*

VAN RIPPER Miss Sabine is a troubled woman. So unlike her sister.

ICHABOD Her sister?

VAN RIPPER Lisbeth Van Fleet.

Pause.

Sabine chose...shall we say...a different path.

ICHABOD I see. She never married?

RIPPER No. It would have been the obvious choice for Baltus to marry the older daughter, but she wouldn't have him as I recall. Very much like her mother, Hilda, in that sense. Gifted but stubborn.

ICHABOD It's charming that the estate has remained in the family for so long. I think it's sad to see so many family run farms selling out to rich plantation farmers from the south!

RIPPER *(agreeing)* Yes. *(He considers this new thought for the* **VAN FLEET** *estate).* *(Business-like)* Excuse me, Mr Crane, I must prepare some papers.

VAN RIPPER *leaves the room.*

[MUSIC NO. 11b: "UNDERSCORE – STRANGE THINGS DO HAPPEN"]

WILLEM Very strange things *do* happen in the Hollow Wood, Mr Crane, but Sabine is a good woman. I've got a lot to thank her for.

ICHABOD *(vaguely interested)* Really?

WILLEM She saved my mother from the smallpox when I was young and even now leaves a basket of medicine on the doorstep whenever one of the family is ill.

ICHABOD Ah! She's an apothecary.

WILLEM Yes, I suppose so...but there are other gifts passed down in that family that aren't so easy to explain.

ICHABOD Such as?

WILLEM Well...no one in the town likes to talk about it, but we all know that Sabine can see things...in dreams...that come true.

KATRINA *enters with a ledger.*

KATRINA Good evening, Mr Crane, Willem.

WILLEM *(awkwardly making it up half under his breath)* So as I was saying, you should see Miss Sabine about that nasty rash of yours. She'll give you something for it I suspect.

KATRINA I've come to deliver the accounts for my father. Where's Herr Van Ripper?

WILLEM He'll be back shortly, Miss.

Pause.

KATRINA *(she leans over to* **ICHABOD** *discreetly)* If you *are* looking for Sabine she's at Mistress Hanneke's tonight. *(Gently)* She won't be there long.

VAN RIPPER *enters.*

RIPPER *(surprised by her unexpected arrival)* Ah, Miss Katrina, what a charming surprise.

KATRINA My mother was unable to come this evening. She sends her apologies and has sent me in her place.

VAN RIPPER Thank you. *(She hands over the ledger and as he takes it he lingers touching her hands)* As it is so late I shall walk you home.

KATRINA Oh, no, there's no need. I am perfectly safe.

VAN RIPPER I would hate for you to be alone.

KATRINA Mr Crane, are you heading home?

ICHABOD I am.

KATRINA There, Mr Crane can see me home as it is on his way. *(To* **ICHABOD***)* Are you ready to leave?

[MUSIC NO. 11c: "TRANSITION – THE GIRL"]

ICHABOD Yes.

They leave.

IMOGEN
SMALL SLEEPY TOWN
FULL OF LIGHT, FULL OF DARK;
ICHABOD CRANE WAS ENCHANTED
BY THE HOLLOW'S HIDDEN SPARK ...

The River Bank

KATRINA *and* ICHABOD *are walking by the river with a beautiful backdrop of fireflies in the long grass.*

ICHABOD Fireflies!

KATRINA They're often by the river this time of year.

ICHABOD Fascinating creatures! I studied them back in Connecticut. They contain some sort of light emitting compound that is activated by a chemical reaction within their biology. Sorry, I'm boring you...

KATRINA No! Not at all. Tell me, do you know *why* they glow?

ICHABOD Well, I think, and I could be wrong, I think...it's actually part of their mating ritual.

KATRINA Oh?

ICHABOD *(scientifically)* The males fly around signalling that they are looking for a mate and the females signal back saying...

KATRINA *(playing him)* Well? What do they say?

ICHABOD *(blushing)* It depends...of course this is only from observation. *(He sees that a firefly is caught in her hair and calmly goes to remove it)* Hold still, there's one caught in your hair.

There is an unintentional intimate moment as ICHABOD *carefully takes out the fly.*

There. *(He takes hold of her hand and puts the fly in it)* What is truly remarkable about the firefly is that they create light with no heat. They are...illuminating!

KATRINA *(breaking away to put down the firefly)* Thank you for walking me home.

ICHABOD Not at all.

KATRINA I am grateful for the company.

[MUSIC NO. 12: "THE TALE OF THE WHIPPOORWILL"]

I feel certain that we will hear the Whippoorwill tonight.

ICHABOD There are many nocturnal birds that sing at dusk... Why is the Whippoorwill so special?

KATRINA Because the Whippoorwill sings as it carries the souls of the dead to heaven.

ICHABOD (*realising who she means*) Ah... Mistress Hanneke.

She nods.

(*considering*) A soul carried on the wings of a bird...it's a beautiful thought.

KATRINA It's not just a thought...

THERE WAS A LITTLE BOY OUT PLAYING AS THE SUN WENT DOWN,
HE COULD SEE THE SHADOWS LENGTHENING AROUND THE TOWN;
AND HE HEARD THE WHIPPOORWILL CALL!
SAID THE LITTLE BOY, 'COME WHIPPOORWILL AND SHOW YOUR FACE!
SING YOUR SONG, AND LEAD ME TO YOUR HIDING PLACE!'
AND SO THE WHIPPOORWILL CALLED!
SHE SANG, 'COME NEAR! COME NEAR! I AM HERE!'

SO THE LITTLE BOY WENT RUNNING TO THE FOREST WILD,
IT WAS COLD AND DARK, HE WAS A FOOLISH CHILD,
BUT HE'D HEARD THE WHIPPOORWILL CALL ...
SOON A RAVEN STOPPED HIM AS HE RAN ALONG,
SAID THE RAVEN, 'BOY, DO YOU NOT LIKE MY SONG?'
'NO!' SAID THE BOY, 'IT IS UGLY AND SHRILL'
I SEEK THE VOICE OF THE WHIPPOORWILL'
HAVE YOU HEARD THE WHIPPOORWILL CALL?
SHE SINGS "COME NEAR! COME NEAR! I AM HERE!"

SO THE JEALOUS RAVEN FOLDED UP HIS WINGS;
'I WILL SHOW THIS CHILD WHERE THE WHIPPOORWILL SINGS.'

SO HE POINTED DOWN TOWARDS A DEEP RAVINE,
THE FASTEST RIVER THAT THE BOY HAD SEEN;
THE BOY HURRIED DOWN TO THE RIVER'S GREAT SOUND;
HE SLIPPED AND FELL, AND THE POOR BOY DROWNED ...

BUT AS HIS SOUL FLEW UP INTO THE COOL NIGHT AIR,
THE SWEET LITTLE WHIPPOORWILL WAS WAITING THERE!
AND SHE CARRIED HIM TOWARD THE SILVER MOON;
ALL THE WHILE, LITTLE WHIPPOORWILL, SHE SANG HER
    TUNE:
CAN YOU HEAR THE WHIPPOORWILL CALL?
SHE SINGS, 'COME NEAR! COME NEAR! I AM HERE!'

They hear the call of the Whippoorwill. **KATRINA** *looks
out.*

ICHABOD *(warmly)* It's just a bird.

KATRINA *(with a sad smile)* I wish I was wrong.

KATRINA *leaves.*

The Van Fleet House – Two

The TENANT FARMERS *have requested an audience with* BALTUS *in his house.* VAN RIPPER *is by his side.*

KLAUS *(cautiously)* Um... Herr Van Fleet...we wondered if we could have a word?

BALTUS What do you lot want now?

KLAUS *(scared)* Umm...

BALTUS Well speak up!!

    KLAUS *is frightened by this and* JOHAN *continues.*

JOHAN We'd like to talk to you about our farms.

    BROM *enters and stands the other side of* BALTUS.

RIPPER What about them?

BALTUS If it's your rotten management then I don't want to hear!

HENRIETTE *(defensive)* How dare you!

    KLAUS *pulls* HENRIETTE *back.*

BALTUS You should learn to control your wife, Klaus.

MARKUS Look, Herr Van Fleet, we have a business proposition for you.

BALTUS That's a long word for you, Markus?! Do you know what it even means?

DRIKA He knows very well what it means, you old... *(Going to say 'crow')*

    MARKUS *silences her.*

BROM Now look, what's going on? If it's about your farms / you can talk to me or Herr Van Ripper.

BALTUS *(interrupting)* My farms!

FLORINA It's more than that, Brom.

RIPPER *(demanding an explanation)* What's this about?

MARKUS We want to *buy* our land!

There is a pause.

BALTUS *starts laughing, which angers the* TENANT FARMERS.

BALTUS *(viciously)* What makes you think you can afford it?

KLAUS We only want to know if there's a chance... *(Seeking support)* Tell him, Brom.

BROM Herr Van Fleet's right, you can't afford it...

DRIKA *(feeling betrayed)* Brom?!

MARKUS No, wait! If we started saving now –

BALTUS Now listen to me, you mules! This land was entrusted to my care by my father-in-law and I'm not about to give it away. If any one of you want out, there are at least twenty other families who'd gladly take your place. Do you hear?

The TENANT FARMERS *cower, defeated.*

Now get out of here! All of you!

They leave.

RIPPER *(after he's watched them leave he turns to* BALTUS*)* If you were to think of selling, there is another option.

BALTUS Well? What is it?

RIPPER It has recently come to my attention that plantation owners from the south are looking to relocate. They're willing to pay a very high price –

BALTUS *(interrupting)* Cotton, is it? I will never sell to a cotton farmer! Those crops strip the land of goodness making it useless within five years. Besides, Hollow Land should be in Hollow Hands!

RIPPER It is merely something to consider.

[MUSIC NO. 13: "UNDERSCORE - AFTER VAN FLEET"]

Move to the **TENANT FARMERS** *who have left the house disheartened.*

HENRIETTE This was a bad idea.

FLORINA *(to* **JOHAN***)* He can't take our farms, can he?

JOHAN He can do anything he pleases.

MARKUS First the bloody school teacher and now this!

FLORINA The Devil never rests!

DRIKA It's all take, take, take! We work our fingers to the bone to line his pockets.

MARKUS Something's got to change.

BROM *follows them.*

[MUSIC NO. 14: "THE PROMISE"]

BROM Wait!

MARKUS What do you want?

BROM You should have come to me first.

HENRIETTE Go away! You know full well that the farms have had another good year. We could save...!

KLAUS Leave it, Hen.

JOHAN Go away, Brom.

FLORINA Go back to the old crow!

DRIKA There was a time you would have stood with us.

BROM There was nothing I could do!

JOHAN He's one of them now.

FLORINA Your father would turn in his grave to see what you've become!

BROM

DON'T THINK FOR A MOMENT I'VE FORGOTTEN WHO I AM;
DON'T THINK FOR A MOMENT I'M NOT JUST LIKE YOU!
DON'T THINK FOR A SECOND THAT I'M NOT THE HOLLOW'S
   MAN, I AM!
I LIVE THE LIFE YOU DO!
ITS EARTH TO HAND AND HAND TO MOUTH;
I KNOW HOW HARD YOU WORK EACH DAY!
COME RAIN, COME SHINE, COME SLEET, COME SNOW,
COME WHAT BLOODY WELL MAY!
MARKUS, HOW'RE THEM PIGS IN YOUR TOP FIELD? THRIVING?

MARKUS

YES, THE LITTER'S DOING WELL.

BROM

GOOD NEWS! JOHAN, HOW'S THAT TOBACCO CROP OF YOURS?

JOHAN

SURVIVING, BUT NEEDS RICHER SOIL AS FAR AS WE CAN TELL.

BROM

TRY POTASH.
AND KLAUS ...
YOU'VE GOT A MARE ABOUT TO FOAL;
GOOD LUCK - MY GIRL DROPPED A FOAL LAST WEEK.

KLAUS

YES!

BROM

IT'S HARD WORK, HARDER THAN YOU'D EVER THINK,
HENRIETTE BETTER BREW A BIT OF GOOD STRONG DRINK!
'CAUSE WHEN THE MORNING FINALLY COMES YOU'LL BE TOO
   DAMN TIRED TO SPEAK.

BUT WHEN YOU SEE THAT FOAL,
WOBBLING ON HIS KNEES;
WHEN YOU SMOKE THAT PIPE
MADE FROM HOMEGROWN LEAVES;

WHEN YOU DRINK YOUR MILK OR COOK YOUR BACON, BREAK
    YOUR DAILY BREAD,
YOU KNOW I KNOW HOW MUCH THAT MEANS!

SO DON'T THINK FOR A MOMENT THAT I'LL LORD IT UP IN
    HERE,
AND PROFIT FROM THE SWEAT FROM OFF YOUR BACKS.
DON'T THINK FOR A SECOND THAT I'M NOT SINCERE;
I WANT A LIFE OF SUN AND EARTH,
NOT ONE OF TITLES, DEEDS AND TAX.

I AM A FARMER, NOT A LANDLORD.
I AM A WORKER, NOT A KING.
TO SEE THE HOLLOW HAPPY,
TO SEE THE VILLAGE THRIVE,
THAT'S WHAT I WANT, MORE THAN ANY OTHER THING.

WHEN THE OLD MAN DIES, THE LAND WILL FALL TO ME.
AND I SWEAR BY EVERY SOUL THAT WALKS THE EARTH:
YOU CAN BUY YOUR FARMS – EVERY ROCK AND EVERY TREE,
THAT'S MY PROMISE, FOR WHAT IT'S WORTH.

MARKUS You'll let us buy the land?

BROM Yes.

KLAUS What do you say, Hen? Do you trust him?

HENRIETTE I don't know...

BROM You've known me all my life. Have I ever let you down?

JOHAN He's got a point.

MARKUS You promise?

   MARKUS *puts his hand out to* **BROM**.

BROM You have my word!

   BROM *shakes* **MARKUS***'s hand.*

MARKUS I reckon that calls for a drink? Don't you?

   Snap to next scene.

Outside the Tavern

[MUSIC NO. 14b: "UNDERSCORE – OUTSIDE THE TAVERN"]

The **TENANT FARMERS** *and* **BROM** *are huddled together talking about* **FATHER ABRAM***'s discussion with* **ICHABOD.**

EVA *is having fun with her friends* **ESTHER, ANNA** *and* **ROSA.**

KATRINA *enters.*

KATRINA Brom. Can I have a word? Now.

BROM *reluctantly goes towards her, away from the others.*

BROM Well? What is it?

KATRINA I've just heard you've promised the tenants they can buy the land when my father dies.

BROM What of it?

KATRINA Does my father know of this?

BROM It's the right thing to do.

KATRINA The right thing? You can't possibly know that...

He goes to leave.

Is that it? Aren't we going to talk about it?

BROM It's business, Katrina, it's not your concern.

KATRINA *(defiantly)* It's *our* business. Yours *and* mine. If you think I'm going to be like my mother, then you are wrong. I don't want that life.

They defiantly hold each other's gaze before **BROM** *leaves.*

KATRINA *goes to talk to* **WILLEM.**

FATHER ABRAM *is talking to the* TENANT FARMERS.

FR ABRAM I tell you! Ichabod Crane is void of any belief...

JOHAN I think we should take all the children out of school!

The all agree except for FATHER ABRAM.

KLAUS He'll never be one of us.

FLORINA What else can we do, Father Abram?

MARKUS I say we chain him up in the Hollow Wood!

They are horrified.

FLORINA He doesn't deserve that!

HENRIETTE *(annoyed)* He's been disrespectful to Father Abram!

JOHAN Calm down, there's nothing we can do tonight.

FR ABRAM That's not entirely true... *(They all look at him)* Since he is so fond of teaching, I say we teach *him* a little history lesson about how *outsiders* are treated in Sleepy Hollow?

ICHABOD *walks in.*

MARKUS *(seeing* ICHABOD *and alerting the others)* Evening, teacher.

Sensing the hostile atmosphere, he walks to WILLEM *and* KATRINA.

The TENANT FARMERS *disperse with a complicity among them.*

ICHABOD Good evening. *(Looking for* VAN RIPPER*)* I thought Herr Van Ripper would be here.

WILLEM He'll be along shortly. Mistress Hanneke died last night, and he had to see to some paperwork.

ICHABOD Last night? *(*ICHABOD *looks at* KATRINA *realising that she was right)* I'm very sad to hear it.

WILLEM Will you be having a drink, Mr Crane?

ICHABOD *(he takes the drink)* To Mistress Hanneke!

They toast Mistress Hanneke while **FR ABRAM** *and* **TENANT FARMERS** *toast their plot to ridicule* **ICHABOD.**

DRIKA Give us a song, Father Abram!

FLORINA Yes! A song for the new teacher!

FR ABRAM *(mock calming the crowd and pretending to be spontaneous)* what a wonderful idea, and how about something from our history since Mr Crane doesn't believe in our 'stories' I'll sing... *(With a mischievous glint in his eye)* The Tale of Major Andre.

The company cheer and get ready for the dance. There is excitement as costume is passed around.

[MUSIC NO. 15: "THE TALE OF MAJOR ANDRE"]

ICHABOD *(to* **JAKOB***)* Who was Major Andre?

JACOB You know! The English soldier in the revolutionary war! He was a spy for the British and he was captured not far from this very spot.

FR ABRAM *(interrupting)* Now, Jakob. Don't go ruining the end!

Villagers act out the various parts, with bits of red and blue fabric denoting Simcoe and Andre. NB: Blue was the colour of the Patriots' uniform in the Revolutionary War, red the colour of the English. **DRIKA** *fetches the coats and chooses* **BROM** *to be Simcoe.*

MAJOR SIMCOE HAD A BRIGHT BLUE COAT,
A COAT AS BLUE AS SKY;
AND YOUNG MISS SALLY TOWNSEND
WELL, THAT COAT DONE CATCH HER EYE!
SO SIMCOE SAID TO SALLY
'I'LL SING A SONG FOR YOU,
IF YOU PROMISE ME TO MARRY
AND TO BE MY LOVER TRUE!'

HE SANG
HEY DIDDLE AYE DIDDLE OH DIDDLE EH!
HEY DIDDLE AYE DIDDLE OH DOH!
HEY DIDDLE AYE DIDDLE DIDDLE OH,
THAT'S THE SONG OF MAJOR SIMCOE!

HENRIETTE – My turn now!

The crowd cheer and lead her to perform.

MAJOR SIMCOE HE WENT OFF TO WAR,
TO FIGHT THE ENGLISH FOE;
AND SALLY IN HIS ABSENCE,
WELL, HER HEART WAS BROKEN SO.
BUT SALLY WAS NOT SAD FOR LONG,
SHE DID WHAT ALL GIRLS CAN;
SHE FIXED HER HAIR ALL PRETTY
AND SHE FOUND AN ENGLISHMAN!

They choose **ICHABOD** *to be* **MAJOR ANDRE.**

DRIKA

MAJOR ANDRE HAD A BRIGHT RED COAT,
A COAT AS RED AS BLOOD;
AND YOUNG MISS SALLY'S PASSION
IT DID FLOWER IN THE BUD!
SO ANDRE SAID TO SALLY,
'FORGET WHAT SIMCOE SAID,
YOU'LL SING THAT SONG FOR TWICE AS LONG
WITH ANDRE IN YOUR BED!'

Outrage and hilarity at the smut.

EVA AND KATRINA

SO SHE SANG:
HEY DIDDLE AYE DIDDLE OH DIDDLE EH!
HEY DIDDLE AYE DIDDLE DALLY!
HEY DIDDLE AYE DIDDLE DIDDLE OH,
THAT'S THE SONG OF YOUNG MISS SALLY!

MEN

OH, HEY DIDDLE AYE DIDDLE OH DIDDLE EH!
HEY DIDDLE AYE DIDDLE DALLY!

HEY DIDDLE AYE DIDDLE DIDDLE OH,
THAT'S THE SONG OF YOUNG MISS SALLY!

FR ABRAM

ONE NIGHT WHEN HE WAS IN HIS CUPS
OLD ANDRE SHOT HIS MOUTH;
HE SAID THE BRITISH ARMY
SOON WOULD ALL BE HEADING SOUTH.
YOUNG SALLY, SHE WAS WRACKED WITH GUILT,
OF SIMCOE NOW SHE THOUGHT!
FOR SOUTH IN SLEEPY HOLLOW,
THAT IS WHERE HER SWEETHEART FOUGHT!

FLORINA/JOHAN

SO SALLY TOOK A PEN AND INK
AND WROTE DOWN ANDRE'S PLAN;
SHE SENT IT OFF TO SIMCOE,
HER YOUNG PATRIOTIC MAN!
SO WHEN THE FILTHY ENGLISH CAME
TO SLEEPY HOLLOW TOWN,
THE PATRIOTS WERE WAITING THERE

ALL

TO SHOOT THE ENGLISH DOWN!

THEY SANG
HEY DIDDLE AYE DIDDLE OH DIDDLE EH!
HEY DIDDLE AYE DIDDLE OH DOO!
HEY DIDDLE AYE DIDDLE DIDDLE OH,
THAT'S THE SONG WE SHOT THEM DOWN TO!

FR ABRAM

MAJOR ANDRE REALIZED ALL AT ONCE
WHAT SALLY'D GONE AND DONE;
HE CURSED THE WOMAN FROM THE END
OF SIMCOE'S LOADED GUN.
AND AS THEY STRUNG HIM UP TO HANG,
THAT FILTHY ENGLISH PIG,
HE TRIED TO SING THIS SONG
BEFORE THE HANGMAN'S JIG:

ICHABOD *is on makeshift gallows, as the villagers dance around him, singing. There are cries of 'Come on, teacher!*

Show us your jig!' etc. and **ICHABOD** *is swept up in the merriment.*

ALL

HE SANG:
HEY DIDDLE AYE DIDDLE OH DIDDLE EH!
HEY DIDDLE AYE DIDDLE OH DAY!
HEY DIDDLE AYE DIDDLE DIDDLE OH,
THAT'S THE SONG OF MAJOR ANDRE!
HEY DIDDLE AYE DIDDLE EH DIDDLE OH!
HEY DIDDLE AYE DIDDLE OH DAY!
HEY DIDDLE AYE DIDDLE DIDDLE OH,

ICHABOD *(as Major Andre) is mock hanged with a bag over his head. The villagers push him off the 'gallows' and he collapses on the floor, terrified by how far this re-enactment has been taken.*

AND THAT'S THE END OF MAJOR ANDRE!

ICHABOD *tries his best to recover and to laugh along with the villagers as* **KATRINA** *helps him up, but he is clearly shaken by the cruel prank.*

HEY DIDDLE AYE DIDDLE OH DIDDLE EH!
HEY DIDDLE AYE DIDDLE OH DAY!
HEY DIDDLE AYE DIDDLE DIDDLE OH,
THAT'S THE END OF MAJOR ANDRE!
HEY DIDDLE AYE DIDDLE OH DIDDLE EH!
HEY DIDDLE AYE DIDDLE OH DAY!
HEY DIDDLE AYE DIDDLE DIDDLE OH,

The dance suddenly goes into slow motion, and we see **ICHABOD** *and* **KATRINA** *brought very close together in a near-embrace.* **BROM** *is watching them. We hear the drumming of hooves, louder, more insistent than before. It rises to a fever pitch, and we suddenly hear:*

SABINE *(voice over)*
CAN YOU HEAR IT, MR CRANE?

Blackout.

ACT TWO

The Street

[MUSIC NO. 16: "THE DREAM"]

It is early morning in Sleepy Hollow, the sky is still dark, and the moon is full. We hear the piercing scream of the **THE INDIAN GIRL.** *Suddenly* **SABINE** *runs into the town. She has awoken from a violent nightmare and is wild with the images still in her head.*

SABINE
I SAW THE HOLLOW IN FLAME;
HOT BREATH OF THE BEASTS OF BURDEN.
I HEARD THEM CALLING HIS NAME
THEIR BELLIES FULL OF WINE!

I SAW THE BLOOD OF MY BLOOD,
HANDS BURNING IN HOLLOW ANGER;
I SAW A CROW WITH A BROKEN WING,
DYING IN THE DARK!

I SEE A SPIDER IN WAIT
THREAD SPUN OVER INK AND PARCHMENT
I SEE THE TWISTING OF FATE
IN A THOUSAND DIFFERENT WAYS!

I SEE THE SPIRITS UNREST
THE HOLLOW WOOD IN ITS DREAD AND GLORY
WE WILL BE PUT TO THE TEST
AND I FEAR THAT WE WILL FAIL!

NOTHING IS CLEAR!
WE ARE ALL CREATURES OF LIGHT AND SHADE,

NOTHING IS CLEAR!
THERE ARE TOO MANY CHOICES THAT MUST BE MADE
A PATH TO LEAVE,
A CHILD CONCEIVED,
A PRICE THAT MUST BE PAID!

I SEE THE HOLLOW IN FLAME;
ONE MAN AT THE BURNING CENTRE;
I HEAR THEM CALLING HIS NAME:
ICHABOD CRANE!

CHORUS *(offstage)*
ICHABOD CRANE!

Suddenly we hear the call of the Whippoorwill. **DRIKA** *appears in her nightgown with a candle. She is listening to the bird knowing that it means death, but who can it be? Then* **FATHER ABRAM** *followed by* **KLAUS** *and* **HENRIETTE** *appear, also in nightwear, then* **FLORINA**, **JOHAN** *and eventually* **MARKUS**. *The* **CHILDREN** *are also coming out.*

SABINE *(babbling to herself)* The Crow...an old crow...crow dying in the dark... Spider... Spider's web... Ink...! Nothing is clear! I see...a path, a child...a price must be paid! *(Crying)* The beasts of burden!

SABINE *has collapsed to her knees.*

[MUSIC NO. 16b: "TRANSITION - AFTER THE DREAM"]

FLORINA Please, Sabine! Some of us are trying to get some sleep!

DRIKA *(to* **MARKUS***)* Did *you* hear it?

MARKUS What?

DRIKA The Whippoorwill?

HENRIETTE I heard it...

FLORINA Who was it calling for?

JOHAN *(looking for answers)* Sabine? Who did the Whippoorwill take? *(Louder)* Sabine?

She does not respond.

FLORINA She can't hear you.

WILLEM *comes running into the town.*

WILLEM Baltus Van Fleet is dead!

The town is in shock. **SABINE** *stares out, lost in her own world, the town murmur among themselves.*

DRIKA It was the old man that the Whippoorwill took.

WILLEM *(to* **FATHER ABRAM***)* Father Abram, Herr Van Ripper has asked for you up at the house.

FR ABRAM Yes, certainly.

FR ABRAM *goes back in to get dressed.*

SABINE
I SAW THE BLOOD OF MY BLOOD,
HANDS BURNING WITH HOLLOW ANGER;
I SAW A CROW WITH A BROKEN WING,
DYING IN THE DARK!

The Van Fleet House – Three

LISBETH *sits as* VAN RIPPER, BROM *and* FATHER ABRAM *make plans.*

FR ABRAM *(to* LISBETH*)* I am sorry for your loss, Herr Van Fleet was a much-respected pillar of our community. He shall be sorely missed.

RIPPER *(to* BROM*)* We need to make plans to remove his body from the house.

BROM When?

RIPPER The sooner the better, if you know what I mean... *(His body will decay)*

BROM *(understanding)* Of course, I'll tell Johan to bring around the funeral cart.

FR ABRAM I will arrange the funeral procession.

RIPPER Something very simple.

FR ABRAM And clothes? What will he be buried in?

RIPPER I'll choose something from his wardrobe...

LISBETH *(the last straw as dressing the body would be something she would do)* Stop...

They look at her.

RIPPER *(comforting)* I understand it's a distressing time, Mistress Van Fleet, but these things must be arranged now.

LISBETH No, no...please, just stop... *(Pause)* Katrina and I will do it...when we are ready...

RIPPER But I need to –

LISBETH *(interrupting)* No... *I* will see to the necessary arrangements.

RIPPER Very well. And the Hallows' Eve Feast?

LISBETH What of it?

RIPPER Perhaps, in light of the circumstances it may be prudent to –

LISBETH The feast will go ahead as planned. My husband wasn't a sentimental man and would have wanted life to continue as it was...besides we may be in need of some distraction.

RIPPER I don't think it's wise –

LISBETH Well, it doesn't matter what you think, it is my house and my decision.

> **ICHABOD** *arrives.* **BROM** *stares at* **ICHABOD** *with pure hatred.*

ICHABOD I'm sorry to intrude, I came to offer my condolences.

LISBETH Thank you, Mr Crane. *(Pointedly)* Herr Van Ripper and Willem are just leaving.

They leave unwillingly.

BROM I'll be back later this morning with Johan, unless there's something else you want me to do.

LISBETH No...you go and see to the farms and bring the cart. I shall make sure he's ready... *(Sudden thought)* And when you go into town will you please tell Herr Van Ripper to make arrangements to read the will as soon as possible. *(Warmly to her future son-in-law)* For the sake of the estate I see no reason to delay.

> **LISBETH** *heads towards the door to usher* **BROM** *out.*

Do *you* know much of farming, Mr Crane?

ICHABOD Not at all.

LISBETH My family looked after the land well, but Baltus made it something more. He was an exceptional land owner. Hollow land in *true* Hollow Hands.

ICHABOD *(surprised)* He descended from the Native Indians?

LISBETH *(insulted)* Certainly not!

ICHABOD I'm sorry, when you said Hollow hands I thought you meant there was some sort of blood connection.

LISBETH *(coolly)* What good is blood?

Pause.

None of us are *entitled* to anything, Mr Crane. The land was long ago inhabited by the...natives, I grant you, but through our hard work and determination haven't we now earned the right to call Sleepy Hollow our own?

KATRINA *enters.*

Katrina. (**LISBETH** *takes* **KATRINA**'s *hand and kisses her on the forehead)*

Pause.

Excuse me, Mr Crane.

LISBETH *leaves to prepare* **BALTUS**'s *body and* **KATRINA** *and* **ICHABOD** *are left alone.*

ICHABOD I'm very sorry for your loss, Katrina.

KATRINA Thank you, but you are probably the only person in the town that is.

ICHABOD I'm sure that's not true.

KATRINA No, it is, and I understand why. He was their landlord... he had to be firm...but to me... *(Faltering with emotion)* to me he showed love and kindness.

ICHABOD He was a good man.

KATRINA No one is wholly good or wholly bad.

ICHABOD I can't believe that's true when I look at you.

They share a moment looking at each.

KATRINA It's good to see you.

ICHABOD I thought you were avoiding me.

KATRINA *(surprised)* No! I haven't been in town much over the harvest and then father being ill...

ICHABOD Yes of course... I'm sorry.

[MUSIC NO. 17: "NOTHING"]

KATRINA What do you think happens after death?

ICHABOD *(he wants to comfort her but is unable to do what is expected)* You know I don't believe in heaven or hell or souls or anything like that. I'm sorry... I can't comfort you with a lie.

KATRINA But what *do* you believe...? What comes next?

ICHABOD
NOTHING.
DARK AND DEEP
SIMPLY NOTHING.
A STARLESS NIGHT,
A DREAMLESS SLEEP ...

NOTHING.
NO JOY, NO FEAR.
THE THINGS WE ARE,
THE THINGS WE WERE
THEY MELT AWAY,
THEY DISAPPEAR.

AND WHAT REMAINS IS GIVEN TO THE EARTH,
OH, KATRINA, THEN, THEN THE WONDERS THAT OCCUR!

KATRINA *begins to echo him.*

ICHABOD	KATRINA
OUR BODIES FEED THE SOIL...	
	OUR BODIES FEED THE SOIL...
THE SOIL GIVES WAY TO GREEN...	
	THE SOIL GIVES WAY TO GREEN...
THE GREEN SHOOTS FEED THE FOREST...	WHICH FEEDS THE FOREST...

BOTH

AND THE FOREST FEEDS THE
FIREFLIES!

NOTHING,
NOTHING COMES FROM NOTHING
EACH BLADE OF GRASS
EACH ROLLING HILL
EACH MIGHTY OAK
EACH WHIPPOORWILL
IS JOINED BY DEATH AND BY BIRTH!
SO LIFE GOES ON ...
LIFE GOES ON.
AND WE, WE MAKE THE EARTH!

On the point of kissing.

ICHABOD We shouldn't.

KATRINA I know.

ICHABOD *steps backwards.*

The Funeral

[MUSIC NO. 18: "THE FUNERAL"]

The scene shifts - a bell tolls. A funeral cortege crosses the stage, and **ICHABOD** *and* **KATRINA** *melt out of their scene to join it. The villagers carry* **BALTUS VAN FLEET**'s *coffin.* **LISBETH** *begins to sing, joined by* **KATRINA** *and* **FR ABRAM.** **SABINE,** *from a distance, joins them:*

LISBETH
SHALL WE GATHER AT THE RIVER?
WHERE BRIGHT ANGEL FEET HAVE TROD?

KATRINA
WITH IT'S CRYSTAL TIDE FOREVER
FLOWING BY THE THRONE OF GOD.

FR ABRAM
YES, WE'LL GATHER AT THE RIVER,
THE BEAUTIFUL, THE BEAUTIFUL RIVER!
GATHER WITH THE SAINTS BY THE RIVER,
THAT FLOWS BY THE THRONE OF GOD!

SABINE
GATHER BY THE RIVER!
THE BEAUTIFUL RIVER!
GATHER BY THE RIVER!

SABINE *walks up and stands next to* **LISBETH.**

LISBETH Why are you here, sister? I know you don't mourn him.

SABINE *(gently)* I'm here for you...for our blood. I fear that history is repeating itself.

LISBETH You just can't bear to think Katrina wants the same life as me. It is her choice.

LISBETH *leaves followed by* **KATRINA, SABINE** *and the rest of the village. The* **TENANT FARMERS** *and* **BROM** *linger in the churchyard. They stare at the mound of* *earth, not knowing who should speak first. Eventually, they begin to sing to* **BROM.**

DRIKA

IT'S A GREAT SHAME
THAT THE OLD MAN'S HAD IT;

WIVES

IT'S A PLEASING LAND,

HUSBANDS

NOW IT SHOULD BE OURS!
IT'S EARTH TO HAND, AND DUST TO DUST;
YOU MADE A DEAL AND WE GAVE OUR TRUST,
WE SOW, WE REAP, WE MADE OUR STAND:
THE TIME HAS COME TO BUY OUR LAND!
SEE, WE MUST BE PART OF SOME ETERNAL PLAN;
EVERY WOMAN, EVERY CHILD AND EVERY SIMPLE WORKING
   MAN.
SO IT'S HAND TO HEART WITH HEAD HELD HIGH,
AS DECENT FOLK WE CAN BUT TRY TO LIVE THE LIFE WE LIVE
AS BEST WE C –

They see **ICHABOD** *and stop abruptly.*

They look at him.

BROM *(getting to the point)* What do you want, teacher?

ICHABOD I was just going to enquire as to why the children haven't returned to school since the harvest?

They look shiftily amongst themselves.

KLAUS It was a busy year...

HENRIETTE There's still a lot for them to do at home for the Hallows' Eve Feast.

ICHABOD So they'll be coming back after that?

They all avoid the question and quickly disperse.

KLAUS We must get going, Hen.

JOHAN I've got to get the funeral cart back to the farm.

DRIKA Espen! Rebekah! Come along, it's time to go.

ENSEMBLE *(offstage)*
ICHABOD CRANE
ICHABOD CRANE
ICHABOD CRANE.

The Reading of the Will

VAN RIPPER's *office in town.* LISBETH, VAN RIPPER, WILLEM, KATRINA *and* BROM.

RIPPER I have here the last will and testament of Baltus Van Fleet. *(Pause)* Perhaps I should point out now that it was made only a few days before the proposed wedding *(he indicates towards* KATRINA *and* BROM*)* ...and in consideration of the event not taking place...the will was rather premature...if you know what I mean.

LISBETH Perhaps it would be best if you read it out loud?

RIPPER Certainly... I only wish to prepare you –

LISBETH *(losing her temper and interrupting)* For God's sake, just read it!

RIPPER Yes, of course.

[MUSIC NO. 19: "THE WILL"]

VAN RIPPER *opens up the document and prepares to read.*

In a separate light BALTUS VAN FLEET *sings the will –* VAN RIPPER *ghosting his words.*

BALTUS *(sung)* / VAN RIPPER *(spoken, gradually fading out)*
I BALTUS VAN FLEET OF THE TOWN OF SLEEPY HOLLOW
BEING OF SOUND MIND AND MEMORY,
BUT CONSIDERING THE MORTALITY OF MANKIND,
DO MAKE AND ORDAIN THIS MY LAST WILL AND TESTAMENT:

TO MY DAUGHTER KATRINA VAN FLEET
AND HER HUSBAND BROM VAN BRUNT
I GIVE AND BEQUEATH THE ENTIRETY OF MY PERSONAL
    ESTATE:
MY DWELLING HOUSE, BOOKS, FURNITURE, WEARING
    APPAREL,
AND THE THREE THOUSAND EIGHT-HUNDRED ACRES OF
    LAND

BETWEEN THE HUDSON RIVER AND THE HOLLOW WOOD
AND ALL PROFITS ARISING FROM IT.

I WILL THAT MY WIFE LISBETH VAN FLEET
SHOULD OCCUPY AND ENJOY ALL AND EVERY PART OF THESE
  DWELLINGS AND LANDS DURING HER NATURAL LIFE.

I CONSTITUTE AND APPOINT HANS VAN RIPPER
AS EXECUTOR OF THIS MY LAST WILL AND TESTAMENT
REVOKING ALL OTHERS HERETOFORE MADE.

VAN RIPPER *(spoken, fading back in)*
SIGNED, SEALED AND DELIVERED IN THE PRESENCE OF
  THE SUBSCRIBING WITNESSES AND AT THE TESTATOR'S
  REQUEST.

WILLEM JANSSEN
HANS VAN RIPPER
BALTUS VAN FLEET
APRIL 3, 1820

LISBETH I don't see what the concern is?

BROM As agreed, the estate belongs to me and Katrina...

RIPPER Ah, but it *doesn't*...

BROM What do you mean?

RIPPER The estate was left to his daughter Katrina and her
  husband Brom Van Brunt, and since you are not yet *married*
  the management of the estate will remain in the power of
  the executor.

BROM Who is...?

RIPPER Me.

Pause as everyone realises what this means.

LISBETH And what exactly do you intend to do with the land?

RIPPER Well... I would continue the work I was doing for Her
  Van Fleet.

LISBETH Which was?

RIPPER Not long before his death he *(thinking how to lie)* 'considered' an enquiry he had from a southern plantation owner wishing to buy the land –

BROM I don't believe it?!

RIPPER Naturally I would retain the house *(he nods to* **LISBETH***)*, but it would be foolish not to pursue such a lucrative offer.

LISBETH But the money will still belong to the estate. What would *you* gain from such an arrangement?

BROM He'll make a deal with the new owners to take a fat percentage! That's what he'll do!!

LISBETH I see! Well...since the wedding will be taking place imminently there will be no need for such an arrangement.

BROM *(to* **KATRINA***)* We could get married tomorrow.

WILLEM Tomorrow's the Hallows' Eve Feast.

BROM So what? The day after then? *(To* **KATRINA***)* We only postponed the wedding because of your father's poor health. There's nothing to stop us now. We can get married as soon as possible! Can't we, Katrina?!

KATRINA has been put on the spot. BROM *can see that she is floundering and realises why.*

It's that bloody school teacher isn't it?

[MUSIC NO. 19B: "UNDERSCORE – AFTER THE WILL"]

KATRINA No! How can you say that?

BROM I've seen the way he looks at you.

LISBETH *(trying to calm him)* Brom.

BROM *(fuming)* I knew from the moment he arrived he'd cause trouble!

KATRINA Please!

BROM I don't believe this! *(Suddenly turning on* **KATRINA***)* How could you break your promise to me? Me! Who you've know all your life!

LISBETH Brom, please!

BROM And you'd force me to break my promise to the tenants?! You'd let him *(meaning* **ICHABOD***)* take everything I've worked for?!

RIPPER *(intervening)* Technically, to inherit the land she can only marry you.

BROM What?

RIPPER The will clearly says 'to my daughter Katrina and her husband Brom Van Brunt'.

BROM *(to* **KATRINA***)* You hear that? To inherit you have to marry me, or else you'll be left with nothing and Ripper will make all the tenants homeless!

RIPPER Now hold on...

BROM Do you want that, Katrina? It's not just about you and me...it's also about them!

Overwhelmed by the confrontation **KATRINA** *runs out.*

(turning to **VAN RIPPER***)* You knew what he meant when he made that will.

RIPPER It was days before the wedding. I had no reason to suspect it would not go ahead.

BROM You did this on purpose!

RIPPER That's not true.

BROM You're a filthy liar!

LISBETH Enough, Brom!

Pause as **BROM** *controls his rage.*

BROM This isn't over!

BROM *storms out of the office and follows* KATRINA.

[MUSIC NO. 20: "DREAM REPRISE – THE FIGHT"]

SABINE

> I SEE THE HOLLOW IN FLAME
> HOT BREATH OF THE BEASTS OF BURDEN
> I HEAR THEM CALLING HIS NAME ...

The scene changes to KATRINA's *walk home along the river bank. Cold and functional in the light of day.* BROM *chases after* KATRINA, *he is fuming; when she sees him she instantly becomes anxious.*

BROM

> ICHABOD CRANE!
> WHY HIM?
> THAT SCRAWNY OUT-OF-
>   TOWNER!
> DOES YOUR HOLLOW BLOOD
>   NOT MEAN A THING?

KATRINA

> *BROM, OF COURSE IT DOES,*
>   *BUT –*

BROM

> TELL ME THE TRUTH,

> *WHAT?*

> HOW LONG?

> *BROM!*

> WHEN DID YOUR EYE START
>   WANDERING?

> *PLEASE!*

> WHAT GOOD DID YOU THINK
>   ALL THIS COULD BRING?

> *BROM, I DIDN'T –*

> YOU'RE JUST CONFUSED,
> YOUR FATHER'S BARELY COLD,
> YOU'RE JUST CONFUSED ...
> I UNDERSTAND,

YOU NEEDED SOMEONE YOU COULD HOLD,
I WASN'T THERE!
I NEVER AM ...

His temper a little calmer, **BROM** *makes a different sort of appeal.*

LOOK, I DON'T KNOW WHAT IT IS I'M SUPPOSED TO DO.
I DON'T KNOW WHO YOU THINK I OUGHT TO BE.
BUT LOOK ME IN THE EYE, KATRINA,
TELL ME PLAIN AND TRUE,
ARE THERE NOT FAR WORSE THINGS THAN A LIFE WITH ME?

I KNOW THAT WE WERE PROMISED VERY YOUNG;
A STRIPLING AND A ROSEBUD SHARING SOIL!
BUT HERE WE BLOODY ARE,
AND LOOK, WHEN ALL IS SAID AND DONE,
WHAT YOU PLANT, YOU TEND,
AND WHAT YOU TEND WON'T SPOIL!

I KNOW WE MAY NOT BE IN LOVE!
BUT YOU MUST UNDERSTAND:
IF WE DON'T SEE THIS THROUGH
THEN THEY WILL LOSE THAT LAND!

KATRINA
Our land!

                              BROM
                              What?

Our land, Brom!
ANSWER ME THIS:
WHAT RIGHT?
TO PLEDGE WITHOUT
    DISCUSSION,
DID YOU THINK THAT I
    WOULD DISAGREE?

                    Why are you bringing this
                    up again?

FATHER WAS MEAN, I KNOW!
HALF THE HOLLOW
    LOATHED HIM,

HOW DO YOU SUPPOSE THAT
    FEELS FOR ME?

This isn't about that!

YES, I'M CONFUSED,
THE GRIEVING LITTLE GIRL,
I AM CONFUSED!

Calm down!

AND YOU STAND THERE ALL
    SELF RIGHTEOUS
AND YOU TELL ME TO BE
    CALM,
BUT YOU'RE ASKING ME TO
    GIVE MY LIFE
FOR SOMEONE ELSE'S FARM!
IT'S NOT INSENSITIVE, IT'S
    STUPID, BROM, I –

BROM *slaps her. They are both still for a second, horrified,
until* **KATRINA** *runs out.*

BROM Katrina!

She does not stop.

The Schoolroom – Three

[MUSIC NO. 21: "PETER, PETER, PUMPKIN EATER"]

The CHILDREN *set up the school during the song but leave, revealing an empty room with* ICHABOD *alone.*

CHILDREN

PETER, PETER PUMPKIN EATER
HAD A WIFE BUT COULDN'T KEEP HER
PUT HER IN A PUMPKIN SHELL
THERE HE KEPT HER VERY WELL

NIGHTLY, NIGHTLY HEAR HER SCREAMING
PETER SLEEPING, NEVER DREAMING
IN THE MORNING, PUMPKIN PIE
WHAT A SHAME SHE HAD TO DIE!

KATRINA *comes into the schoolhouse and sees* ICHABOD *sat alone.*

KATRINA Where are all the children?

ICHABOD They've stopped coming to school. *(*ICHABOD *paces around the classroom as if he's trapped)*

KATRINA Why?

ICHABOD At first, I thought it was because of the harvest.

KATRINA That was weeks ago...

ICHABOD But then I realised it was Father Abram and the parents trying to force me out because I can't believe their silly stories!

KATRINA *(affectionately)* Oh, Ichabod... Why do you still question everything?

ICHABOD *(suddenly turning on her)* And why do you question nothing?!

KATRINA What do you mean?

ICHABOD You know what I mean.

KATRINA No, I don't!

ICHABOD *(openly)* Can't you feel it?

KATRINA I can feel that things aren't as they should be.

[MUSIC NO. 22: "TRANSITION - SCHOOLROOM - THE GIRL REVEALVED"]

ICHABOD *(hurt)* Is that all?!

KATRINA I would have been happy to marry Brom and inherit the estate –

ICHABOD *(heated)* So do it! Marry Brom!

KATRINA It would be a good life, but nothing in the world can ever change what's true!

ICHABOD And what's that?

KATRINA That I don't feel about him the way I feel about you.

Pause.

(with no intention of leaving) I knew I shouldn't have come here.

ICHABOD *(giving her a last opportunity to do the right thing)* It's not too late to leave.

They look at each other.

KATRINA I don't want to.

KATRINA *rushes towards* **ICHABOD** *and they kiss as darkness falls on them.*

IMOGEN *appears in a separate light.*

IMOGEN
MY MOTHER USED TO SAY
THAT NOTHING IN THE WORLD
CAN EVER CHANGE WHAT'S TRUE.

SHE DIDN'T DO THE RIGHT THING
BUT DOES THAT MAKE IT WRONG?
AND MY FATHER ...
MY FATHER ...

CHORUS

POOR CHILD
POOR THING!
HER MOTHER IS COLD IN THE CHURCHYARD
AND STILL THE WHIPPOORWILL
WON'T SING ...

The Van Fleet House – Four

> BROM *and* VAN RIPPER *are in a heated debate over the estate.* LISBETH *and* WILLEM *are also in the room.*

RIPPER ...It is the right thing to do!

BROM Where will we live?

RIPPER You'll still have your farm.

BROM But what about them?

RIPPER Brom, you have to put the needs of the many ahead of the needs of a few. With better industry and trade, more people will come here. Sleepy Hollow will become prosperous and we will all benefit.

> KATRINA *arrives home slightly dishevelled. They all stare at her when she comes in.* VAN RIPPER *and* BROM *try to control* KATRINA *throughout the scene.*

BROM *(suspicious)* Where've you been? I was worried...

KATRINA I just went for a walk.

LISBETH *(getting to business)* Herr Van Ripper's plantation owner wants to buy the estate within the week.

KATRINA Within the week?

BROM Tell him we're getting married...

RIPPER *(to* KATRINA*)* You'll still have the house, and the farm that Brom manages now...it will just be the land and the small farms...

BROM *(to* KATRINA*)* The tenants' farms!

RIPPER *(to* KATRINA*)* New York is getting bigger by the day, and the demand on food and clothes is greater than ever! Until now our trade has been low but with this sale you can help make Sleepy Hollow a thriving centre of industry.

BROM *(ignoring him and with contempt)* By letting some outsider come in and profit from the land we've tended these past two hundred years?!

WILLEM The land wasn't ours to begin with...

BROM Well it's ours now.

RIPPER *(to* **KATRINA***)* I'm not asking you to make a decision to marry Brom. I'm asking you to see that this sale is good for the whole town.

BROM Don't listen to him!

RIPPER Your father would have wanted it.

BROM He'd never have sold to a cotton farmer! Much less a southerner!

RIPPER It's the right thing to do!

BROM Katrina! Marry me and put an end to all this nonsense!

RIPPER You don't have to do that...

KATRINA *(making a decision)* I know what I need to do...

LISBETH Stop!

[MUSIC NO. 23: "THE POWER"]

They all look at **LISBETH***.*

Pause as **LISBETH** *considers what to do.*

I wish to have a word with my daughter. Alone. You can wait in the study.

Reluctantly they leave.

KATRINA *(with maturity)* You didn't need to send them out.

LISBETH
WHEN DID YOU GROW UP?
WHEN DID YOUR CHILDHOOD DISAPPEAR?
WHEN DID YOU GROW UP?

WHEN DID THE PASSING OF A DAY
BECOME THE TURNING OF A YEAR?
HOW CAN HAVE YOU GROWN INTO A WOMAN
WHO HOLDS THE HOLLOW'S FUTURE IN HER HAND?
YOU HAVE SUCH POWER IN THIS
BUT DARLING, PLEASE UNDERSTAND ...

THE CHOICES THAT WE MAKE,
THEY CAN FEEL NOBLE AND FEEL STRONG.
BUT WE SIMPLY NEVER KNOW, WE NEVER KNOW
UNTIL THOSE CHOICES HAVE BEEN MADE,
IF THEY WERE RIGHT OR THEY WERE WRONG!
NOTHING IN THE WORLD IS EVER CERTAIN,
SO NONE OF US CAN TELL YOU WHAT TO DO
YOU HAVE THE POWER IN THIS
MY DARLING CHOOSE WHAT YOU MUST,
BUT CHOOSE FOR YOU.

KATRINA *goes to the door to usher* **BROM** *and* **VAN RIPPER** *back into the room.* **LISBETH** *is unaware that* **KATRINA** *has realised the only way to escape is to run away.*

BROM *and* **VAN RIPPER** *come in.*

KATRINA Gentlemen, I have decided to follow my father's wishes...and marry Brom. *(She half-heartedly smiles at* **BROM***)* Since tomorrow is the Hallows' Eve Feast, and to my mind an inappropriate day to have a wedding, I propose we marry the day afterwards. If you agree?

BROM I agree.

BROM, RIPPER *and* **WILLEM** *leave.*

As the music starts there is a moment between **KATRINA** *and* **LISBETH**. **KATRINA** *indicates that she is up to something.*

[MUSIC NO. 24: "HALLOWS' EVE – THE HEADLESS HORSEMAN"]

The scene shifts from the previous scene, leaving **KATRINA** *alone on stage. It is Hallows' Eve. Preparations are beginning for the festivities – pumpkins being lit, food and drink being laid out. The house is warm and bright, secure from the cold and the darkness outside.* **EVA** *enters.*

MEN
AT THE CENTRE OF THE HOLLOW WOOD

KATRINA Eva! I need you to take this message to Ichabod.

EVA *(imploringly)* Katrina, how can you ask me that?

KATRINA Please, as my *friend*...

EVA But Brom is my *brother*!
THERE STANDS A MIGHTY TREE

KATRINA It's not what you think... I'm telling him I can never see him again...that he has to leave.
THEY SAY THAT HE IS BURIED THERE

EVA All right. If I go now I can be back before dark.
HIS BODY ROTS

KATRINA Thank you. (**KATRINA** *hugs her with relief*)
BUT HIS SPIRIT'S FREE ...

In another part of the house.

WOMEN
THEY SAY HE WAS AN ARMY MAN

LISBETH Willem, the mist is coming in quicker than I thought... perhaps you should light the torches now, so everyone can find their way.
WHO SLEW THE BLACK-EYED GIRL

WILLEM I don't like it.

LISBETH Everything will be alright.

At the gates of the house...

ALL

THEN LOST HIS HEAD

MARKUS I've locked the gates all around the wood.

ON HOLLOW SOIL

BROM Good, it feels like we're expecting a storm.

NO RECOMPENSE

We don't want any cattle bolting.

FOR BLOODY TOIL
SO HE RIDES!

MEN

YOU HEAR HIM AS THE SUN GOES DOWN!

WOMEN

A THUNDER IN THE GLOOM

ALL

NO FENCE OR GATE
CAN BAR HIS WAY
YOU DREAD THE NIGHT AND RUE THE DAY
THAT HE RIDES!

We are at the party. **VAN RIPPER** *takes over the telling of this last part – a ghoulish re-enactment for the entertainment (and horror) of the* **CHILDREN**, *who squeal with delight.*

VAN RIPPER

THE FLANKS OF HIS STEED ARE ALL SPECKLED WITH SWEAT
ITS EYES ARE DILATED IN PAIN
AS HE PUSHES THE ANIMAL ON, FASTER YET,
A SPEED NO ORDINARY BEAST COULD SUSTAIN!
POUNDING THE EARTH WHERE HIS OWN BLOOD WAS SHED
NOT SLOWING NOT STOPPING FOR BREATH;
HE SEEKS THE REMAINS OF HIS SEVERED HEAD!

IF YOU SEE HIM, WHEN YOU SEE HIM
MUTTER YOUR PRAYERS IN THE DARKNESS,
IT CAN MEAN ONLY DEATH!

Cheers.

VAN RIPPER *enjoys the moment and* BROM *comes forward and offers his hand.* VAN RIPPER *shakes his hand in the knowledge that he has been defeated.*

BROM *calms down the crowd calling their attention for a speech. He is keeping a firm hold on* KATRINA *and is still mistrusting of her.*

BROM I know I'm not one for making speeches, but I feel that tonight calls for me to say a few words.

EVA *(shouting)* Make it quick, we want to dance!

The crowd laughs.

BROM I shan't be long. *(Raising his voice)* Are all the doors bolted?

JOHAN *nods his head.*

Now, as all of us here knows, we shut ourselves away on Hallows' Eve to protect ourselves from the spirits roaming the Hollow Wood. But while we think of those from the past, let us also remember those here in the present, and those that *may* come in the future. *(He looks to* KATRINA *as there is a suggestive cheer in the crowd)* And let us be grateful that at this moment in time, come what may, there's warmth...drink...and life!

[MUSIC NO. 24b: "UNDERSCORE – PARTY MUSIC – WHIPPOORWILL"]

The crowd cheers and disperses into groups, laughing and having fun. LISBETH *is heading over to* KATRINA *and* BROM *and gets stopped by a child showing her a pumpkin.*

RUTH What do you think?

LISBETH Very scary!

ABEL Why are they called Jack-O'-Lanterns?

LISBETH They're named after a very bad man! Actually, my mother used to sing a song about it.

RUTH Will you sing it?

LISBETH Soon. Why don't you go and put that pumpkin down with the others?

Across the room.

FLORINA *(to her* **CHILDREN***)* Now remember to stay inside tonight! You don't want to be seeing The Headless Horseman, do you?!

MARTHA *(defiantly)* I don't believe he's real!

FLORINA Do you want to go and find out?

MARTHA No.

FLORINA Then do as you're told!

> **KATRINA** *watches the festivities glumly.* **BROM** *observes her melancholy behaviour and approaches her.*

BROM Come on, Katrina! Would you at least dance?

KATRINA *(aware of how she must look)* I'm sorry. Yes. *(Turning to* **LISBETH***)* Mother, I think it's time for a song.

LISBETH *(aside to* **KATRINA***)* Are you sure.

KATRINA Yes. I'm sure.

BROM It's time for another song, everyone!

> **LISBETH** *squeezes* **KATRINA***'s hand affectionately and walks to the centre of the room as the crowd shush each other for silence.*

[MUSIC NO. 25: "THE TALE OF THE DRUNKARD JACK"]

LISBETH

ONE STORMY SUMMER'S EVENING, THE DEVIL CAME TO TOWN
HE WAS HUNTING SOULS TO JOIN HIM ON HIS JOURNEY WAY
    BACK DOWN.
HE CALLED OUT TO THE SINNERS, ALL PARALYZED WITH
    FEAR:
HE SAID 'OLD NICK'S COME TO GET YOU, SO FORM A LINE
    RIGHT HERE!'

FIRST HE TOOK THE MISERS, WHO WOULD NOT SHARE THEIR
    GOLD,
THEN HE TOOK THE MISANTHROPES WHOSE STONY HEARTS
    WERE COLD.
THE HYPOCRITES WERE NEXT, THEY DIDN'T PRACTICE WHAT
    THEY PREACH;
THERE'S NOT A SOUL ON GOD'S GREEN EARTH THAT'S OUT OF
    SATAN'S REACH!

BUT IN THAT CONGREGATION, THERE WAS A MAN NAMED
    JACK;
A DRUNKARD BOUND FOR HADES WITH HIS SINS UPON HIS
    BACK.
HE SAID,

MARKUS

'MY DEAREST LUCIFER, I'LL JOIN YOU WILLINGLY,
IF YOU PICK ME AN APPLE FROM THAT THERE APPLE TREE.'

ALL

JACK! JACK! DRUNK ON SIN;
PLAYING WITH THE DEVIL, YOU CAN NEVER WIN!
GAMBLING YOUR ETERNITY ON AN APPLE FROM AN APPLE
    TREE!

JOHAN

THE DEVIL SMILED HIS DEVIL SMILE AND SAID
'AN APPLE? FINE!
I'VE PLENTY OF EXPERIENCE WITH APPLES IN MY TIME.'
HE CLIMBED THE TREE, BUT ALL AT ONCE OLD NICK WAS AT A
    LOSS;

MARKUS

> FOR JACK HAD DRAWN HIS HUNTING KNIFE AND CARVED A
> MIGHTY CROSS!

JOHAN

> 'A CROSS?' THE DEVIL WEPT AND WAILED, 'I CANNOT COME
> DOWN NOW!'
> HE STAMPED HIS CLOVEN HOOVES UPON THE CREAKING
> APPLE BOUGH.

MARKUS

> SO JACK SAID, 'TELL YOU WHAT, MY FRIEND, JUST SIGN THIS
> LEGAL SCROLL;
> I'LL LET YOU COME BACK DOWN TO EARTH IF YOU LET ME
> KEEP MY SOUL!'

ALL

> JACK! JACK! DON'T YOU KNOW?
> WHAT YOU REAP IS WHAT YOU SOW?
> RISKING YOUR ETERNAL SOUL WITH YOUR NAME UPON A
> LEGAL SCROLL!

LISBETH

> SO LUCIFER CONCEDED, JACK WALKED AWAY WITH GLEE.
> HE LIVED A LIFE OF DRINK AND SIN, FOOTLOOSE AND FANCY
> FREE.
> BUT WHEN IT CAME HIS TIME TO DIE ...

ALL

> ST PETER SAID:

FR ABRAM *(spoken)* 'You're barred!'

LISBETH

> THE DEVIL HE LAUGHED LONG AND LOW AND THE TRUTH IT
> HIT JACK HARD.

At some point during the song **KATRINA** *leaves followed
by* **EVA**.

JOHAN

'I CLIMBED YOUR TREE', THE DEVIL CRIED, 'I SIGNED YOUR
    STUPID SCROLL!
YOU HAVE IT THERE IN WRITING THAT I CANNOT TAKE YOUR
    SOUL!
IF HEAVEN WILL NOT HAVE YOU, WELL, YOU CAN'T STAY HERE
    WITH ME;
YOU'LL WALK THE EARTH IN DARKNESS, FOR ALL ETERNITY!'

MARKUS

'NOT THAT', SAID JACK ON BENDED KNEE, 'I CANNOT BEAR
    THE DARK!'
'HOW WILL I SEE MY WAY WITHOUT A CANDLE OR A SPARK?'

JOHAN

SO SATAN PLUCKED AN EMBER FROM HIS FIERY PIT OF WOES,
AND STUCK IT IN A PUMPKIN –

ALL

A PUMPKIN?

LISBETH/JOHAN/MARKUS

A PUMPKIN!
THAT'S HOW THE STORY GOES!

ALL

JACK JACK! NE'ER DO WELL;
CAN'T GO TO HEAVEN AND CAN'T GO TO HELL!
DOOMED TO WALK ETERNAL NIGHT WITH A PUMPKIN AS
    YOUR ONLY LIGHT!
JACK JACK! A TALE TO TELL!
COULDN'T GO TO HEAVEN AND COULDN'T GO TO HELL
DOOMED TO WALK ETERNAL NIGHT WITH A PUMPKIN AS HIS
    ONLY LIGHT!

LISBETH Thank you, thank you! There is food and drink laid
out next door and when the feasting is over there shall be
more dancing!

*[MUSIC NO. 25b: "UNDERSCORE – PARTY MUSIC
– PETER, PETER"]*

They cheer in their merriment and there is movement on stage as they gather more drink, dance etc. **BROM** *looks around for* **KATRINA.**

DRIKA *(enjoying the party)* Who wants a dance, with me?!

MARKUS *(already drunk he grabs her around the waist)* I will... after I've had a pork pie.

DRIKA You'll dance with me, won't you, Brom? If Katrina doesn't mind! Katrina? Where is she?

BROM I don't know. *(Calling out)* Katrina?! And where's my sister? *(To* **JOHAN***)* Have you seen her?

JOHAN Jakob, go see if you can find them.

JAKOB *leaves.* **VAN RIPPER** *sees the commotion and whispers to* **WILLEM** *to search outside.* **WILLEM** *leaves.*

BROM *(to* **LISBETH***)* Where is she?

LISBETH Who?

BROM Katrina!

LISBETH I thought she was with you.

BROM And Eva?!

LISBETH I don't know, Brom.

JAKOB *rushes back in.*

JAKOB I can't find them anywhere.

BROM *turns on* **LISBETH.**

BROM This is your doing, in't it?

LISBETH I don't know what you mean.

BROM *(angry)* Where has she gone??

RIPPER *(pulling him back)* Stop this now.

BROM Oh! You... *(Outraged)* !! *(To* **LISBETH** *and* **VAN RIPPER***)* Are you in this together?

WILLEM *enters and runs to* **VAN RIPPER.**

WILLEM Herr Van Ripper!

RIPPER What is it, Willem?

WILLEM I saw Miss Katrina heading out towards the Hollow Wood and Miss Eva was following her.

BROM *(mad)* I will not let her make a fool of me!

JOHAN Calm down, Brom.

BROM You don't understand! We have to get Katrina back.

KLAUS What do you mean?

BROM *(pointing at* **RIPPER***)* Are you going to tell them or shall I?!

RIPPER This isn't the time or the place.

BROM *(at fever pitch to the whole crowd)* If I don't marry Katrina then *he's* going to sell your farms out from under you.

There is confusion and uproar **JOHAN** *- 'What?',* **KLAUS** *- 'He can't do that!' -* **DRIKA** *- 'To who?'*

BROM Some bloody plantation owner from down south!

RIPPER *(trying to justify his actions)* It's the best thing for Sleepy Hollow!

HENRIETTE *(to* **RIPPER***)* My family have lived in that farm for over a hundred years!

BROM If we leave now we can stop her at the Hollow Wood. *(A few quietly gasp and* **BROM** *sees their terrified faces)*

JOHAN You want us to go out *there*?

BROM If you want to keep your farms you'll have to.

The **TENANT FARMERS** *talk amongst themselves and quickly prepare to leave.*

JOHAN *(to* **FLORINA***)* We've got to try.

HENRIETTE *(to* **KLAUS***)* No one ever goes out on Hallows' Eve!

KLAUS *I know.*

DRIKA Where's Markus?

They find **MARKUS** *slumped in a drunken stupor.*

DRIKA *(shaking him)* Get up, Markus!

FLORINA You stay here, children. Do you understand? Don't leave the house!

HENRIETTE *(surprised)* Are we going?

BROM Klaus, get as many lanterns as you can!

They leave with their lanterns.

LISBETH *(calling after them)* Brom! It's madness! Let her go! *(Accusing* **VAN RIPPER***)* This was your fault! You forced them into this!

RIPPER *(bemused)* It was just business.

LISBETH *(distraught)* What do you think they'll do when they find them?

RIPPER *(a moment of decision)* I can make this right. *(Calling off)* Willem, fetch a lantern.

They leave.

[MUSIC NO. 26: "THE LETTER"]

KATRINA/ICHABOD
MY DARLING ICHABOD,
PLEASE FORGIVE ME
I HAVE LIED AND I HAVE DECEIVED,
I DO SO EVEN NOW.

POOR EVA THINKS THIS LETTER MARKS THE END OF MY LOVE
FOR YOU.

WE MUST AWAY FROM THE HOLLOW TONIGHT.
TOMORROW THEY THINK I WILL MARRY BROM,
BUT I WILL NOT, I CANNOT!
MY MOTHER UNDERSTANDS;
SHE WILL HELP US SLIP AWAY.
MEET ME ON THE HIGH ROAD
AS THE BELL STRIKES TEN;
FROM THERE WE WILL TRAVEL THROUGH THE HOLLOW
WOOD.
BY DAWN WE WILL HAVE LEFT THIS PLACE
FAR BEHIND US.

KATRINA Be safe. Your loving Katrina.

By the end of the letter we see **ICHABOD** *alone at the edge
of the Hollow Wood, he hears the voices of* **BROM** *and
the* **TENANT FARMERS** *calling out for him.*

The Hollow Wood

[MUSIC NO. 27: "THE HOLLOW WOOD"]

From offstage.

BROM Take the next path to the right.

JOHAN We can't get to the bridge, it's flooded!

We see a flash of **THE INDIAN GIRL**. **ICHABOD**, *thinking it to be* **KATRINA**, *calls out.*

ICHABOD Katrina!

When the figure emerges, we see it is **SABINE**.

SABINE
I SEE THE HOLLOW IN FLAME
HOT BREATH OF THE BEASTS OF BURDEN
I HEAR THEM CALLING HIS NAME
ICHABOD CRANE!

ICHABOD *makes a move to enter the Wood...*

ICHABOD Are you here to stop us too?

SABINE The Hollow Wood isn't safe! Choose a different path!

ICHABOD It's the only way. I am not afraid.

He goes into the wood. **SABINE**, *alone, suddenly hears the drumming of hooves.*

SABINE
I SEE THE SPIRITS, UNREST
THE HOLLOW WOOD IN ITS DREAD AND GLORY

She vanishes into the wood.

Another part of the Wood

KATRINA *is waiting for* ICHABOD, *but* EVA *has caught up with her.*

EVA You're *here* to meet *him*, aren't you?!

KATRINA Leave us alone.

EVA You lied to me!

KATRINA Brom would have killed him.

EVA It's *Hallows' Eve*, Katrina, it's not safe!

KATRINA We have no other choice.

They hear more shouts from the distance 'Crane! Katrina!'

Go back, Eva!

KATRINA *heads off into the wood.* EVA *decides to follow.*

More hoofbeats are heard as BROM, FATHER ABRAM *and the* TENANT FARMERS *arrive at the edge of the wood. The mist is thick now and it is hard to see where the road ends and the wood begins.*

DRIKA Do you hear that?

MARKUS It's coming from the North.

JOHAN No, East!

They look wildly around them trying to find the source of the sound.

BROM This way!

BROM *leads them into the wood.* SABINE *watches them enter.*

SABINE

WE WILL BE PUT TO THE TEST
AND I FEAR THAT WE WILL FAIL ...

Another flash of **THE INDIAN GIRL.**

ICHABOD Katrina?

THE INDIAN GIRL *vanishes;* **ICHABOD** *and* **SABINE** *follow her into the Wood.*

[MUSIC NO. 27B: "UNDERSCORE - THE HAUNTING"]

An eerie stillness. **ICHABOD**, *alone, hears muttering, whimpering.*

Poor Little Tom

He sees a silhouette in the shadows. A child. The whimpering continues.

TOM *'Yea, though I walk through the valley of the sh- ...of the sh- ...'*

ICHABOD Hello? Are you lost?

The child turns around, a Bible in his hand, blood pouring from his face. It is the ghost of **POOR LITTLE TOM.**

TOM Mother? Mother?

CHORUS (VOICE OVER)

POOR LITTLE TOM SHOULDA LEARNED HIS LETTERS!
POOR LITTLE TOM SHOULDA TAKEN HEED!

ICHABOD *recoils in horror and the child vanishes.*

The drumming of hooves is heard as the wood twists itself around to another location.

Major Andre

BROM *and the* **TENANT FARMERS** *are creeping through the wood, clearly terrified.*

There is a strange creaking sound, like the swinging of a rope.

Suddenly, from the canopy of trees there swings the body of a man in a red coat.

CHORUS (VOICE OVER)
MAJOR ANDRE HAD A BRIGHT RED COAT
A COAT AS RED AS BLOOD!
HEY DIDDLE AYE DIDDLE OH DIDDLE EH ...
THAT'S THE END OF MAJOR ANDRE!

Again, the drumming of hooves, and the wood twists into a new location.

Peter Pumpkin Eater's Wife

EVA *and* **KATRINA** *arrive. Without warning, a figure of a woman rises up from the earth dressed all in white. She is holding two halves of a smashed pumpkin with juice mixed with blood dripping from her hands and clothes. She screams a long, high-pitched scream...*

NIGHTLY NIGHTLY HEAR HER SCREAMING
PETER SLEEPING NEVER DREAMING
IN THE MORNING PUMPKIN PIE
WHAT A SHAME SHE HAD TO DIE!

The apparition returns to her grave. Once more we hear the drumming of hooves, closer this time.

[MUSIC NO.27c: "THE HORSEMAN"]

KATRINA I have to find Ichabod.

EVA There isn't time! The Horseman!

KATRINA (*thrusting her bag towards* **EVA***)* Take my bag, there is food and money. Go! Leave Sleepy Hollow forever! Save yourself!

The hoofbeats are even closer now, almost deafening. **EVA** *flees.*

ICHABOD *emerges from another part of the wood. He rushes to* **KATRINA** *and embraces her.*

Can you hear it?

ICHABOD Yes!

BROM *and the* **TENANT FARMERS** *approach from one side. They are all wild-eyed, terrified – they have seen horrors. They surround* **KATRINA** *and* **ICHABOD***.*

As they talk, the trees behind them twist into the shape of the White Oak. The hoofbeats continue.

BROM Katrina!

KATRINA We just want to be together, Brom!

BROM You know why that can't happen.

FLORINA Without you, we lose everything!

DRIKA This is your home, Katrina. Our home.

BROM You must marry me, Katrina, no matter what.

ICHABOD Keep away, Brom, she's chosen a life with me!

JOHAN Never! Her place is here, in Sleepy Hollow.

MARKUS Hollow Land should stay in Hollow Hands!

In a flash, **THE INDIAN GIRL** *runs across the stage –* **ICHABOD** *starts, and as he moves, the* **TENANT FARMERS** *launch themselves at* **KATRINA***, wrenching her away from him. In the same instant, a terrifying whine is heard, the unholy shrieking of an animal in pain.* **ICHABOD**

finds himself alone in the clearing, face to face with
THE HEADLESS HORSEMAN.

CHORUS *(as the voice of the* **HORSEMAN***)*
ICHABOD CRANE!
ICHABOD CRANE!
ICHABOD CRANE!

*The monstrous apparition vanishes back into the White
Oak, and as the* **TENANT FARMERS, BROM, FATHER
ABRAM, SABINE, WILLEM, LISBETH** *and* **VAN RIPPER**
emerge from the smoke and mist, they find that **ICHABOD
CRANE** *has vanished.*

[MUSIC NO. 28: "THE CURSE"]

KATRINA
ICHABOD! ICHABOD! NO!
WHAT HAVE YOU DONE WITH HIM?
ICHABOD! ICHABOD! PLEASE!
WHERE DID HE GO?
YOU DID THIS, YOU DID THIS!
WHY?
WHAT HAD HE DONE TO YOU?
ICHABOD! ICHABOD!
I DO NOT HEAR THE WHIPPOORWILL CALL,
THE WHIPPOORWILL CALL!

SO ...
DOES HE LIVE? DOES HE LIVE?
HOW?
WHERE DID THE HORSEMAN TAKE HIM?
YOU DID THIS, YOU DID THIS,
WHY?
BECAUSE HE WAS NOT ONE OF US!
HYPOCRITES, HYPOCRITES!
'DECENT FOLK WE CAN BUT TRY TO
LIVE THE LIFE WE LIVE AS BEST WE CAN!'

THE INDIAN GIRL *appears in the shadows and approaches*
KATRINA *as she sings.*

WE ARE ALL CREATURES OF LIGHT AND SHADE;
WE LIVE AS BEST WE CAN!
BUT LOOK AT THE CHOICES THAT WE HAVE MADE;
OUT OF PRINCIPLE OR PRIDE;
FOR A PROMISE OR A KISS,
AND WE SIMPLY COULDN'T KNOW
THAT THEY WOULD LEAD US ALL TO THIS ...!

SO,
HERE WE ARE! HERE WE ARE!
YOU, TRYING TO MAKE ME STAY,
WELL!
HERE I AM, HERE I AM,
NO REASON NOW TO GO!
HOLLOW LANDS, HOLLOW HANDS, FINE!
TAKE EVERY BLASTED ACRE!
BUT THIS ONE THING YOU MUST KNOW ...

SINCE YOU HAVE ROBBED US OF THE CHANCE TO LEAVE THE
    HOLLOW
THEN I MUST WISH THE SAME ON YOU.
FOR ALL YOUR DEATHS AND EVERY DEATH THAT IS TO
    FOLLOW,
THE WHIPPOORWILL WILL NEVER SING;
NO SOUL WILL RISE UPON HER WING,
THE DARK WILL FALL ON EVERYTHING!

WE WILL JOIN THE SPIRITS OF THIS HAUNTED WOOD,
AND OUR SOULS WILL STAY IN SLEEPY HOLLOW ... FOR GOOD.

Back To 1833

IMOGEN *and* JOSHUA *are outside the church.*

IMOGEN *(continuing the story)* After that night the people of Sleepy Hollow kept their distance from my mother. Perhaps it was because they felt guilty of what they had done, or perhaps it was out of fear, not knowing if the curse was real or not. The next day my mother married Brom Van Brunt who fulfilled his promise and sold the land to the tenant farmers. Perhaps my mother *could* have found some sort of happiness with Brom, we will never know.

JOSHUA Why? What happened?

Unobserved, EVA, *now in her thirties, has overheard the end of this conversation. She is dressed in the latest fashion from New York.*

IMOGEN Not long after I was born, the town was plagued by yellow fever. My mother hid us away in the Hollow Wood, where no one else dared to go. I think she was comforted by the thought that my father might be nearby. When we eventually came back into the town, most of the people she knew, including Brom, had died.

JOSHUA And did the Whippoorwill sing?

IMOGEN Not once...

[MUSIC NO. 29: "EVA REMEMBERS – THE TALE OF THE INDIAN GIRL"]

Sometimes I close my eyes and pretend that I'm back in the Sleepy Hollow of my mother's stories. I pretend that the burnt down schoolhouse is still there and that I can share lessons with the other children. I like to imagine what the Midsummer Fair was like, and how it would feel to catch a real firefly with my bare hands...

EVA

> A PLEASING LAND OF DROWSY CHARMS
> OF DREAMS THAT DANCE BEFORE THE HALF-SHUT EYE
> OF HONEST HEARTS AND OPEN HANDS
> ALL SOMEHOW TWISTED WITHOUT KNOWING WHY.

JOSHUA *holds his mother's hand.*

You must be Imogen.

IMOGEN And you are Eva Van Brunt.

EVA Mrs Hoffman now, and I see you've met my son, Joshua.

IMOGEN They said it was all my mother's fault.

EVA You mustn't think that, Katrina wasn't solely to blame, neither was Brom or Ichabod...

JOSHUA Then who?

EVA

> YEARS AGO
> BEFORE THIS LAND WAS OURS
> THERE WAS A GIRL
> AN INDIAN CHILD.
> SHE WARNED HER TRIBE
> OF THE WHITE MAN'S THREAT
> BUT NO ONE LISTENED.
>
> SO WHEN THEY CAME
> TO MAKE THIS LAND THEIR OWN
> THE POOR GIRL RAN
> AND HID WITHIN THE HOLLOW WOOD.
> THEY SAY SHE DIED,
> CUT DOWN BY THE HORSMAN'S HAND
> AND THERE SHE STAYS.
>
> SINCE THAT DAY
> SINCE THAT DAY HER BLOOD SOAKED THE SOIL
> SHE'S WATCHED US THRIVE
> HERE ON THE LAND HER FATHERS OWNED;
> PERHAPS AT LAST,

SHE TOOK REVENGE FOR WHAT SHE LOST
BUT WHO CAN SAY ...?

Would you like to come home with us?

IMOGEN There is nothing for me here.

EVA *puts out her hand, which* **IMOGEN** *gratefully holds.*

*As they leave Sleepy Hollow for good the trapped souls
sing from the shadows as the* **THE INDIAN GIRL** *stands
surveying her land.*

CHILDREN

SHALL WE GATHER AT THE RIVER
WHERE BRIGHT ANGEL FEET HAVE TROD?
WITH IT'S CRYSTAL TIDE FOREVER
FLOWING BY THE THRONE OF GOD

YES WE'LL GATHER BY THE RIVER
THE BEAUTIFUL, THE BEAUTIFUL RIVER
GATHER WITH THE SAINTS BY THE RIVER
THAT FLOWS BY THE THRONE OF ...

End

ABOUT THE AUTHOR
Helen Watts

Helen trained at Italia Conti on the BA Acting (Hons) course.

After a few years of working as an actress Helen moved to writing and directing, with a particular interest in 19th century classic literature. Adaptations for stage include *Persuasion, Far From The Madding Crowd, Northanger Abbey, Under The Greenwood Tree, Frankenstein: The Year Without A Summer* and *A Christmas Carol*. Book-writing commissions include *Lysistrata* (Royal Central School of Speech and Drama); *The Legend Of Sleepy Hollow* (National Youth Music Theatre) and *Mrs Beeton Says...* (Bristol Old Vic Theatre School). Directing credits include *Persuasion, Daisy Pulls It Off* and *Mary Shelley* (Arts University Bournemouth); *Così Fan Tutte* and *Stone Cold Murder* (Dorset Corset Theatre Company) and *Love Is Not A Science* (Royal Central School of Speech and Drama).

Helen is Artistic Director of Dorset Corset Theatre Company and lives in the West Country with her family.

ABOUT THE COMPOSER AND LYRICIST

Eamonn O'Dwyer

Eamonn is an Associate of the Royal Academy of Music and has worked as a musician, composer and sound designer in theatres all over the world. He has written original music for *Mrs Beeton Says...* (Bristol Old Vic Theatre School); *The Legend Of Sleepy Hollow* (National Youth Music Theatre, The Other Palace); *The Comedy of Errors* and *Julius Caesar Re-imagined* (RSC, Swan); *Flesh & Bone* (National Theatre Studio); *Grimm Tales* and *Peter Pan* (Chichester Festival Theatre); *Improbable Fiction* (Mill at Sonning). He is a frequent musical collaborator at the Rose Theatre in Kingston, where he has written original songs and scores for *Hansel & Gretel*, *Alice in Winterland*, *The Wind in the Willows*, *The Lion, The Witch & The Wardrobe*, *A Christmas Carol*, *Hamlet*, *Tess of the d'Urbervilles* and *Arabian Nights*. The score for his original musical *The House of Mirrors & Hearts* won the *MTM* Award for Best New Score at the Edinburgh Festival in 2010, and after its critically acclaimed run at the Arcola Theatre in 2015 has now been performed in Australia and the US.

Other plays by HELEN WATTS & EAMONN O'DWYER
published and licensed by Concord Theatricals

Mrs Beeton Says...

FIND PERFECT PLAYS TO PERFORM AT
www.concordtheatricals.co.uk